THE HISTORIC PRINCIPLE

OF THE

INDISSOLUBILITY OF MARRIAGE

According to the Doctrine and Discipline
of the Anglican Communion

BY

EDWARD B. GUERRY, LL.B., S.T.M.

Rector of the Parishes of St. James, James
Island, and St. John, John's Island
and Wadmalaw Island, South Carolina.

FOREWORD
BY
The Rt. Rev. H. St. George Tucker, D.D.
FORMER PRESIDING BISHOP

THE UNIVERSITY PRESS
THE UNIVERSITY OF THE SOUTH
Sewanee, Tennessee, 1953

Copyright 1953
By Edward B. Guerry
Charleston, South Carolina

DEDICATION

To the Memory of My Brother
SUMNER GUERRY
1892—1951
Priest and Missionary
Always Loyal to the Highest
Teachings of the Church

FOREWORD

MR. GUERRY'S THESIS is a clear and able exposition of the principle of the indissolubility of marriage. He shows that, according to our Lord's teaching, it is grounded in God's creative purpose. The New Testament indicates its acceptance as a basic moral requirement by His early followers. After tracing the history of the attitude of various branches of the Church towards this principle during the centuries which followed, Mr. Guerry demonstrates its wholehearted acceptance by the Anglican Communion. Our own branch of that Communion has, however, in its recent legislation shown a tendency towards compromise, or at least confusion, in its attitude towards the principle. Mr. Guerry, therefore, concludes his Thesis by advocating the need for a statement demonstrating clearly our adherence to the historic doctrine and discipline of the Anglican Communion.

I heartily commend the reading of this Thesis to the clergy and laymen of our Church. Law is the application of a principle to concrete situations. While there may be differences of opinion as to the process of application, we do need to be careful that it does not involve disloyalty to the principle itself, but is a step forward toward its understanding and acceptance by human society.

H. St. George Tucker
Former Presiding Bishop of the Protestant Episcopal Church in the U. S. A.

PREFACE

THIS THESIS has been written in such a manner that the busy clergyman or layman will be able to find herein, all set out for his convenience, the relevant Biblical and canonical passages, a short summary of the sources of our Lord's sayings, the views of some modern scholars on the subject with copious quotations from their writings, selected statements by the Joint Commissions on Marriage and Divorce of the General Convention, etc. I have endeavored to set forth as fairly as possible the different opinions of various scholars, and also, of course, to substantiate my position. For permission to use the many quotations which I found necessary in order to do this, I am indebted to the authors and publishers whose names are indicated by an asterisk in the Bibliography.

My purpose is to bring out in bold relief against the background of the historic Anglican doctrine the confusion and inconsistencies of popular and liberal thought now existing in the Church. Thus, I may cause others to rethink their positions. Out of this might come another great book like Canon Lacey's *Marriage in Church and State*.

It is difficult to express adequately my gratitude to all of the interested persons who have helped and encouraged me in this task. However, I should like to mention a few. My primary inspiration has been my father, the late Rt. Rev. William A. Guerry, D.D., eighth Bishop of South Carolina, who inculcated in me, while I was yet in my boyhood, the principle of the indissolubility of marriage. The Rt. Rev. Albert S. Thomas, S.T.D., retired Bishop of South Carolina, who ordained me to the diaconate and to the priesthood, has supplied me with numerous publications of the Joint Commissions on Marriage and Divorce and with Canon Lacey's book. His firm convictions concerning the indissolubility of marriage have been a constant source of strength.

Next, I am profoundly grateful to the University of the South, Sewanee, Tennessee, and its Graduate School of Theology, for the opportunities which it has afforded. This Thesis was written for my degree of Master of Sacred Theology. I am also indebted to Dr. M. Bowyer Stewart and Dr. Pierson Parker of the General Theological Seminary in New York for their counsel and criticisms. My gratitude is extended to Miss Harriet E. Coffin of Charleston, South Carolina, for her patience and zeal in the very difficult task of deciphering and typing my handwritten manuscript.

Finally, my indebtedness includes my beloved wife; without her interest and co-operation I could never have completed this task.

EDWARD B. GUERRY

St. Mark's Day, 1952

P.S. After my Ms. was in the process of being set up in type, it came to my attention that the Rt. Rev. R. C. Mortimer, D.D., the Bishop of Exeter, had revised Canon Lacey's *Marriage in Church and State*, and that the same had been published in 1947 by the S. P. C. K. I have inserted into the text references to this edition and have indicated where a revision has been made. It is important that our Bishops, clergy, and other interested persons have this book in their possession for study and reference.

October 1952   E. B. G.

INTRODUCTION

THE thesis of this book is the indissolubility of marriage according to the doctrine and discipline of the Anglican Communion throughout the world. The position of this Communion concerning this question rests firmly on the general teaching and practice of the One, Holy, Catholic and Apostolic Church of all Christendom of the first centuries of the Christian era before the time of the Justinian influence on the Church in the East, the medieval and modern innovations of the Holy Roman Church, and the renunciation of the apostolic faith of the Ante-Nicene and Post-Nicene Church, in its Catholic and Biblical completeness, by Protestantism.

This is true not only of the doctrine of marriage but of the other essential teachings and practices of this Church. The Lambeth Conference Committee on the Unity of the Church (1948) has said: "The Anglican Communion may in general terms be described as a portion of the Holy Catholic Church, independent of the Latin and Oriental branches of the Church, maintaining the Nicene faith and the historic order of ministry and sacraments. . . . It is continuous in all things essential with the primitive Church."[1]

This being so, it is unnecessary for the American Episcopal Church or for any other national branch of the Anglican Communion to look to Rome or Constantinople (The Eastern Orthodox Churches) for any real or determining guidance on the problem of marriage and divorce. Unfortunately, this approach to the question has been taken on more than one occasion by the Joint Commission on Holy Matrimony of the General Convention. Our own Anglican tradition and practice concerning marriage and divorce is by far the most reliable and has, with few

---
[1] *The Lambeth Conference* 1948, p. 78.

variations and a minimum of confusion, the best record of faithfulness to the mind of Christ according to the practice and interpretation of the Early Church.

The truth of the indissolubility of marriage is clearly set forth in The Form of Solemnization of Matrimony in The Book of Common Prayer, which is a part of Article X of the Constitution of the American Episcopal Church. This is a point which should be constantly borne in mind, for it signifies that this principle is an organic part of the fundamental doctrine of our Church, which can be changed only in accordance with required constitutional procedures. As this service is also a part of The Book of Common Prayer according to the use of The Church of England, the principle of indissolubility is an essential teaching of that National Church. We should remember that our American Episcopal Church has explicitly declared her steadfast intention not "to depart from The Church or England in any essential point of doctrine, discipline, or worship."[2]

It is, however, a matter of primary importance that we fully grasp what this principle of indissolubility signifies from the standpoint of its historic use during the past two thousand years of Church history, for it is possible to admit the truth of this doctrine and then, either by word or practice, deny its real meaning. It is obvious to careful students of what has been happening in our Church in this respect since 1946 that this has actually been taking place. There are those who so circumscribe, with specious reasoning, this fundamental truth about marriage and family life that the principle itself is in effect repudiated.

Not until we understand anew the teaching of The Book of Common Prayer on marriage, which is the historic position of this Church, can we reliably interpret the new marriage canons of the General Convention (1946), especially on the very in-

---

[2] The Book of Common Prayer, p. vi.

tricate problem of the remarriage of divorced persons by the American Episcopal Church.

If we are unable to interpret them properly, or if divergent interpretations are permissible, then the application and administration of these Canons by the Bishops of our Church, with any degree of unanimity, becomes an impossibility. The disastrous result will be that the American Episcopal Church will not speak with a unified voice of authority and clarity concerning the teaching of our Lord and Saviour Jesus Christ on this subject.

Involved in all of this is the integrity of the family, that great public institution, which is the basic unit of society and the very cornerstone of our civilization. Historically, the principle of the indissolubility of marriage, as affirmed by our Lord, is the original and divine law of the Eternal Father and Creator of all men, upon which the family depends for its existence, security, and perpetuation.

CONTENTS

	PAGE
DEDICATION	III
FOREWORD	V
PREFACE	VII
INTRODUCTION	IX

CHAPTER I

PRELIMINARY CONSIDERATIONS	3
1. Definition and Explanation of Terms	3
a. Divorce *a Mensa et Thoro*	3
b. Divorce *a Vinculo Matrimonii*	3
c. A Decree of Nullity	4
d. The Function of the Church	7
e. A Valid Secular Marriage and a Christian Marriage	9
f. The Indissolubility of Marriage	11
2. The Crux of the Problem before the Church	11
3. Confusion in the Church	15

CHAPTER II

THE MIND OF CHRIST ON MARRIAGE AND DIVORCE	25
1. The Reliability of the Sayings of Jesus concerning Marriage and Divorce	25
2. The New Testament Passages	29
3. Some Modern Viewpoints on the Mind of Christ	35
a. The School of Divorce	36
b. The School of Indissolubility	50
4. An Evaluation	68

CHAPTER III

	PAGE
THE HISTORIC POSITION OF THE ANGLICAN COMMUNION ON THE INDISSOLUBILITY OF MARRIAGE	87
1. The Ante-Nicene Church—To the time of Constantine and the Council of Nicaea 325 A.D.	88
2. From Constantine to Justinian 314-527 A.D.	89
3. The Middle Ages—From the time of the Justinian Code (542 A.D.) to the Reformation	90
4. From the English Reformation to the Present Day	95
5. The Church of England and the Pauline Privilege or Prerogative	100
6. Lambeth on Marriage	106

CHAPTER IV

AN HISTORICAL SKETCH OF MARRIAGE LEGISLATION IN THE AMERICAN EPISCOPAL CHURCH	115
1. From 1808 to 1925	115
2. From 1925 to 1946	118

CHAPTER V

THE NEED FOR A STATEMENT ON THE INDISSOLUBILITY OF MARRIAGE ACCORDING TO THE DOCTRINE AND DISCIPLINE OF THE ANGLICAN COMMUNION	133

APPENDICES

A. THE ADMISSION OF DIVORCED PERSONS TO HOLY BAPTISM, CONFIRMATION, AND HOLY COMMUNION	143
B. THE PASTORAL CARE OF THE BISHOP UNDER CANON 18, SECTION 2(B)	148

CHAPTER I

PRELIMINARY CONSIDERATIONS

1. DEFINITION AND EXPLANATION OF TERMS
   a. Divorce *a Mensa et Thoro*
   b. Divorce *a Vinculo Matrimonii*
   c. A Decree of Nullity
   d. The Function of the Church
   e. A Valid Secular Marriage and a Christian Marriage
   f. The Indissolubility of Marriage
2. THE CRUX OF THE PROBLEM BEFORE THE CHURCH
3. CONFUSION IN THE CHURCH

PRELIMINARY CONSIDERATIONS

1. Definition and Explanation of Terms.

WE must be precise in our use of relevant terms, e.g., divorce, judicial separation, nullity, etc.; or else endless confusion will ensue.

a. *Divorce* a Mensa et Thoro.

Literally, this means a decree of judicial separation from bed and board, which relieves, for proper cause, the husband and wife from the obligation of cohabitation. It does not attempt to dissolve the *vinculum matrimonii* (the bond of marriage) and gives substantially every relief which a decree of absolute divorce affords, except the right of remarriage. It was granted from time to time by the old ecclesiastical courts of England, and, after 1857, by the secular court of that country. The Church has never raised any insuperable objection to such legal action when a husband and his wife find it impossible to live together in comparative peace and harmony. In the United States this decree is obtainable in the various states under common law procedures in the absence of any statutory provisions.

"Divorce, in the second sense above mentioned, viz., judicial separation, has always been admitted as justified in certain cases."[3] Canon Lacey says that "it may be said generally that any conduct of husband or wife making cohabitation intolerable, and frustrating the true ends of marriage, is considered sufficient ground for the exercising of the dispensing power, in the form of a judgment of divorce.[4] Theologians commonly reduce these causes to the three heads of adultery, apostasy, and grave peril to soul or body."[5]

---

[3]A. T. Macmillan, *What is Christian Marriage?* p. 87.
[4]In his book he uses the word "divorce" to mean only "divorce *a mensa et thoro.*"
[5]T. A. Lacey, *Marriage in Church and State*, p. 98; Revised Edition, p. 84 (For "divorce" the word "separation" is substituted).

b. *Divorce* a Vinculo Matrimonii[6]

This is an attempt by a civil or ecclesiastical court to dissolve the bond of matrimony itself, so that the parties to the dissolved marriage are free to remarry. Such a decree definitely recognizes that a valid and true bond of marriage has existed with all of the enduring relationships of husband and wife, parents and children, yet it declares that the marriage is dissolved for causes which have arisen since the inception of the same. In nearly all cases it shuts forever the door of reconciliation.

Divorce *a vinculo matrimonii* signifies this today in Western Christendom but in the old ecclesiastical divorce or matrimonial courts of England, which were abolished in 1857 and their functions turned over to the secular court, it meant only a decree of nullity; for divorce, i.e., the attempted dissolution of the valid and true bond of marriage for causes arising after its formation, was not then known or recognized.[7]

c. *A Decree of Nullity.*

This is a declaration by a civil or an ecclesiastical court that a valid and true bond of marriage was never created due to the existence of impediments *ab initio*, which vitiated the consent necessary to the formation of the relationship of marriage.

The ministers of a marriage are the parties thereto. Therefore, it has long been held, due to the influence of the old Roman law, that anything which prevents the giving of voluntary and free consent to the contract of marriage nullifies the marriage, or, in other words, keeps the bond of matrimony from being formed. "The Christian Church for many centuries simply accepted and conformed to the Roman law and Roman customs so far as was compatible with Christian views[8] commonly confirming the union by religious benedictions. Now it cannot be

---
[6] From the bond of matrimony.
[7] See MacMillan, *op. cit.*, p. 86.
[8] There was no conformity on the principle of indissolubility.

too clearly stated that in the Roman law the one essential feature of marriage was the mutual consent of the parties."[9] If the bond of matrimony is never formed, there is not and never was a marriage between the parties. A decree of nullity is simply a recognition of this fact and gives the persons involved the right to contract a marriage or marriages.

Consent to a marriage is also vitiated by an unlawful union, e.g., an incestuous marriage. One cannot consent lawfully to an illegal union.

The necessary elements of consent and other requirements considered essential by Biblical and ecclesiastical law for the creation of a valid bond of holy matrimony are aptly summarized by Canon Lacey:

> These five conditions, then, are required for a valid contract of marriage. The parties must intend true marriage; they must be physically capable; they must be acting freely, under no constraint and under no mistake; they must be subject to no previous bond of marriage; and they must not be too near akin.[10]

Father Joyce says:

> Christians would appear from the very first to have hallowed their marriages by acts of religion. The Church gave her solemn benediction to the bridal pair: the Mass formed the chief feature of the nuptial celebration. References to the part taken by the priest or bishop in the solemnization of Matrimony occur from the second century onwards. But ... the Church taught that the constitutive factor of marriage lay, not in the benediction, but in the mutual consent of the partners, and that this sufficed to form a marriage even though no priest were present. Throughout the Middle Ages she enjoined the public religious celebration of marriage with ever increasing stringency and

---
[9] O. D. Watkins, *Holy Matrimony*, p. 78.
[10] *Op cit.*, p. 32. Revised Edition, p. 28.

under pain of grave ecclesiastical penalties. But even where her commands were flouted, she did not question the validity of the union.[11]

There are two classes of impediments which affect seriously the consent necessary to a true marriage, i.e., diriment impediments and voidable, or prohibitive, or obstructive impediments.[12] The former render a marriage void *ab initio*. Such an impediment, when it occurs *ab initio*, existed at the inception of a marriage and often continues to exist, thus coming entirely under the alternative wording of Canon 18, Section 2 (b), "to exist or to have existed." No willingness on the part of the parties to the marriage can do away with this type of impediment and thereby render such a union valid. Such diriment impediments are, for example: marriages of an incestuous nature or a marriage with a person hopelessly insane *ab initio*.

On the other hand, voidable impediments do not nullify *ipso facto* a marriage. Only one of the parties, however, involved in the marriage has the right to enter such a plea of nullity; no one else can take advantage of a voidable impediment. This type of impediment, while not rendering the marriage absolutely void, makes it a sinful or irregular or undesirable union; e.g., a marriage which results from mistaken identity or duress. These impediments may also be set up by some legislative authority and may deal with non-essential requirements and formalities.

A party having the right to enter a plea for nullity on the basis of a voidable impediment must act within a reasonable time after he possesses information concerning the same; or else, he will be estopped from alleging on the basis of it that he has not thereafter truly consented to the marriage in question; for example: public cohabitation in family life (not mere sexual intimacy) over a period of time or even years, during

---

[11] G. H. Joyce, S. J., *Christian Marriage*, p. 103.
[12] MacMillan, *op. cit.*, p. 110 and Lacey, *op. cit.*, p. 113. Revised Edition p. 96.

which he should have acted on his ground of annulment, having known about it all the time, constitutes prima facie evidence that the original consent which was vitiated by the impediment—whether it be fraud, duress, mistaken identity, concurrent contract of concubinage or for a trial marriage,—has actually been replaced by the genuine consent necessary for the formation of a true and valid bond of marriage. In other words, a relationship which was not originally a valid marriage can become one unless the offended party moves promptly. *A Marriage Manual*, edited by Bishop DeWolfe, says:

> Thus, there is no marriage in the case of a diriment impediment; there cannot be marriage in the case of a prohibitive impediment *unless the latter limitation can rightly be accepted by both parties, and is actually so accepted.**[13]

We must bear in mind clearly the important distinction between the terms "nullity" and the modern significance of "divorce *a vinculo matrimonii.*" "A decree of nullity ought not to be called divorce, because it is a declaration that in point of fact there has been no binding contract."[14]

The principle of nullity is adequately recognized in the Form of Solemnization of Matrimony in the Book of Common Prayer:

> If either of you know any impediment, why ye may not be lawfully joined together in Matrimony, ye do now confess it. For be ye well assured, that if any persons are joined together otherwise than as God's Word doth allow, their marriage is not lawful.

d. *The Function of the Church.*
It is three-fold:
(1) To witness publicly to the contract of marriage between

---
*Italics mine.
[13]P. 7.
[14]Lacey, *op. cit.*, Preface p. X.

the parties thereto, who are the ministers thereof. Actually they marry each other. The witness and the blessing of the Church are not essential to the formation of a valid marriage in the eyes of God, although Church members cut themselves off from sacramental grace, when they are married by secular officials only.

(2) To give the blessing of the Church through the priest, which is the initial sacramental grace of Christian marriage.

(3) To protect and to uphold the sanctity of marriage with its lifelong obligations. This includes every valid bond of matrimony. The Church is concerned not only with the happiness of the individuals who are the parties to a marriage, but also with the perpetuation of the bond of marriage and the interests and welfare of the children. We can safely say that the Church is chiefly concerned with the family; not merely with the contentment of individuals who enter into marriage. It is generally acknowledged (certainly by the Catholic Churches) that the Church is just as much concerned about marriage as the State is, and, therefore, has the right of spiritual jurisdiction over its members.

St. Paul begins his passage on marriage in I Cor. vii with the words: "Now concerning the things whereof ye wrote. . . ." This means that as the Apostle of Christ he was telling them in response to their inquiry, how our Lord, according to his interpretation, expected them to conduct themselves in regard to marriage and divorce. "And unto the married I command, yet not I, but the Lord. . . ."[15] Here we have an early example of the assertion by a great apostle of the Church's right of spiritual jurisdiction over her members in regard to this matter. After referring to this Pauline passage, Canon Lacey feels sure that, during this early period, "there was an incipient Canon Law of Marriage, enforced by the discipline of the Church.

---

[15] I Cor. 7:10.

From the age immediately succeeding that of the Apostles, there survives one clear indication of such disciplinary control: 'It is proper,' writes St. Ignatius, 'for those intermarrying to effect their union under the direction of the bishop, that their marriage may be after the Lord and not after their own lust'. . . .'[16]

The Church does not seek to govern those who are outside of her fold, or to hand down rulings concerning matrimony affecting the parties, unless one or both of them are members or are about to become members of the Church. When unbelievers, however, have been married outside of the Church, and afterwards become believing members, the Church assumes spiritual jurisdiction over their marriage.

e. *A Valid Secular Marriage and a Christian Marriage.*

In these modern days, it is popular to make quite a distinction between a valid monogamous marriage entered into by persons not Christians and a marriage entered into by Christians before a priest of the Church.

For the present, suffice it to say:

(1) All marriages between baptized Christians, unless subject to a decree of nullity, are valid marriages, and the parties thereto recipients of sacramental grace.

(2) If Christians are married by a secular official, their marriage is, nevertheless, a valid marriage and subject to the spiritual jurisdiction of the Church.

(3) A marriage entered into by unbelievers or by the unbaptized, being in the order of nature, is valid, though without the sacramental grace of Christian marriage. It is a grave error to assume that all such marriages are mere contracts of concubinage, or are of a temporary or trial nature, so as to render

---

[16]*Op. cit.*, p. 117. Revised Edition, p. 100. *Ad Polycarpum*, 5.

all such contracts of marriage inconsistent "with the contract constituting canonical marriage."[17]

We have some very good authority for this statement:

> ... care must be taken to insist on the fact that *true marriage is not a peculiar institution of the Christian Church.** The teaching of our Lord recalls men and women to God's design, and His grace will enable them to rise up thereto; but marriage contracted without Christian rites must be regarded as sacred, and the contracting parties led to recognize the dignity and obligations of the estate on which they have entered. (Report of the Joint Commission on Legislation on Matters Relating to Holy Matrimony, *Journal of the General Convention*, p. 503, 1916, and signed by these Bishops: Jos. B. Cheshire of North Carolina, A. C. A. Hall of Vermont, F. Burgess of Long Island, C. P. Anderson of Chicago; also Mr. Frederic C. Morehouse.)
>
> Christians therefore have in the tradition of the Church a fuller exposition of the divine law of marriage, as it is in the order of nature, than can be found elsewhere. Christian marriage is not a particular kind of marriage, though there is superadded to the marriage of Christians a certain quality ... by which it becomes sacramental. There is not a less perfect marriage common to all men, and a more perfect marriage proper to Christians. Marriage is true marriage alike in the Christian, in the pagan, and in the creedless theist or atheist who has renounced Christianity. In so far as marriage is better ordered in Christendom, it is only as Christians know and observe more fully than other men the natural law of marriage. ... To break away from the Christian tradition is not to return to nature; it is to fall back upon a less-developed knowledge of nature.[18]

Our Lord Himself seemed to have implied an approval of this position, for his remarks according to St. Mark, Ch. 10 and St.

---

[17] See Impediment 8, *infra* p. 13.
*Italics mine.
[18] Lacey, *op. cit.*, p. 34. Revised Edition, p. 30 (cf. *id.*, pp. 48 ff.).

Matthew, Ch. 19, were not addressed to Christians but to Jews who were not his disciples. "Christ is in the first instance addressing Jews, and showing from Jewish Scriptures[19] that their own marriages are indissoluble."[20]

In accord: The Lambeth Committee on the Church's Discipline in Marriage: "Our Lord did not constitute a new kind of marriage; He recalled men to what, by God's law, marriage had always been, that is to say, a lifelong relationship between one man and one woman to the exclusion of all others."[21]

(4) The Impediment known as Disparity of Cult or Religion is not recognized by the Church of England.[22]

f. *The Indissolubility of Marriage.*

This term is used repeatedly in this Thesis, and, therefore, its precise meaning should be defined. It signifies that the bond of marriage constitutes a relationship which can only be dissolved by death. According to the doctrine of Christ, it can no more be destroyed than the other relationships which arise out of marriage; e.g., father and son, brother and sister, etc. Of course, much else in marital and family relationships, such as love, mutual confidence and respect, etc., is dissoluble; in short, the personal relationship of man and wife can be severely impaired or even completely destroyed. The fact or bond of matrimony, however, abides as a lifelong status or relationship, and carries with it the obligation to remain loyal and to be prepared always for reconciliation.

2. THE CRUX OF THE PROBLEM BEFORE THE CHURCH.

The crux of the problem before the Church on this vital issue is the remarriage of divorced persons for causes arising or developing after a former marriage or marriages. The

---

[19]The reference here is to the natural law as set forth in Gen. 2:24.
[20]Dr. Stuart L. Tyson, *The Teaching of Our Lord as to the Indissolubility of Marriage*, p. 78.
[21]*The Lambeth Conference* 1928, p. 103.
[22]See MacMillan, *op. cit.*, pp. 51 and 82; *infra*, p. 101.

Canon on this matter is Canon 18, especially Section 2 (b), which includes the list of impediments to marriage set forth in Canon 17, Section 2(b). These sections read as follows:

> Canon 18, Sec. 2 (b): If the Bishop or Ecclesiastical Authority is satisfied that the parties intend a true Christian marriage he may refer the application to his Council of Advisors, or to the Court if such has been established by diocesan action. The Bishop or Ecclesiastical Authority shall take care that his or its judgment is based upon and conforms to the doctrine of this Church, that marriage is a physical, spiritual, and mystical union of a man and woman created by their mutual consent of heart, mind and will thereto, and is a *Holy Estate instituted of God and is in intention lifelong; but when any of the facts set forth in Canon 17, Section 2, Clause (b), are shown to exist or to have existed which manifestly establish that no marriage bond as the same is recognized by this Church exists, the same may be declared by proper authority.** No such judgment shall be construed as reflecting in any way upon the legitimacy of children or the civil validity of the former relationship.
>
> Canon 17, Section 2. No Minister of this Church shall solemnize any marriage unless the following conditions are complied with: . . . .
>
> > (b) He shall have ascertained the right of the parties to contract a marriage according to the laws of this Church, and not in violation of the following impediments:
> >
> > > 1. Consanguinity (whether of the whole or of the half blood) within the following degrees:
> > >   a. One may not marry one's ascendant or descendant.
> > >   b. One may not marry one's sister.
> > >   c. One may not marry the sister or brother of one's ascendant or the descendant of one's brother or sister.

---

*Italics mine.

2. Mistake as to the identity of either party.
3. Mental deficiency of either party sufficient to prevent the exercise of intelligent choice.
4. Insanity of either party.
5. Failure of either party to have reached the age of puberty.
6. Impotence, sexual perversion, or the existence of venereal disease in either party undisclosed to the other.
7. Facts which would make the proposed marriage bigamous.
8. Concurrent contract inconsistent with the contract constituting canonical marriage.
9. Attendant conditions: error as to the identity of either party, fraud, coercion or duress, or such defects of personality as to make competent or free consent impossible.

Closely related to Canon 18, Section 2(b), is Canon 17, Section 6, which directs that no minister of this Church shall solemnize the marriage of a divorced person, "except as hereinafter in these Canons provided." This refers to Canon 18, Section 2(b). The identical prohibition applies to any member of this Church who plans to marry a divorced person.[23]

Canon 16, Section 3, (a) and (b), which deal with the admission of divorced persons to Holy Baptism, Confirmation, and Holy Communion, are also intimately related to Canon 18, Section 2(b). However, the manner in which the Church should deal with persons who have entered into marriages which are not allowed by the Word of God and the discipline of this Church, is primarily a problem of a disciplinary nature, and not one as to whether or not the Church can afford to bless, at its inception, a marriage which is unlawful in the eyes of God and of the Church. The former case presents the Church with an accomplished fact. Nevertheless, laxity in the appli-

---

[23] See Canon 17, Section 6.

cation of Canon 16, Section 3, (a) and (b), seriously weakens the position of the Church and we deal with this problem of discipline in Appendix A.[24] This matter, however, can be of importance only if the essential principle of indissolubility is preserved in connection with the remarriage of divorced persons. It is with this primary, fundamental and all-important issue that we are chiefly concerned. If the historic position of the Anglican Communion can not be held here, then all is lost, and it could be justifiably said that there would remain very little reason or need to have any canons at all governing the remarriage and also the discipline of divorced persons.

So the central and underlying principle of the canons on marriage and on the remarriage of divorced persons must be clearly perceived, understood, and universally applied throughout the American Episcopal Church. The same should be so for the whole Anglican Communion in connection with the underlying principle of the Form for the Solemnization of Matrimony in The Book of Common Prayer.

We shall go astray if we attempt to read into the Canon on the remarriage of divorced persons what we, as human beings, think God's will, as revealed in Christ, ought to be or should be. *The only safe method is honestly to rediscover what God's will is according to "the Discipline of Christ, as the Lord hath commanded, and as this Church hath received the same"** (Prayer Book, p. 542.); and then proceed to apply His divine principle or law in the faith that God knows human nature better than we do and has planned for the perpetuation of the family in the best possible manner. St. John Chrysostom once said:

> "Read not to me the laws which have been enacted by those without, the laws commanding to give a bill of di-

---

[24]*Infra*. p. 143.
*Italics mine.

vorce, and to put away. For in that Day God will not judge thee by those laws, but by the laws which He Himself has imposed."[25]

In reaching a solution for this involved problem, we need the guidance of the historic voice of the Anglican Communion. The opinions of individuals, valuable as they are, can not alter the essential doctrines of the Faith, once for all delivered to the Saints. It is obvious also that such an alteration can not be brought about by the General Convention through the adoption of mere canons. The principle of indissolubility is one of those essential doctrines of the faith because the family is the unit of society. It is perfectly expressed in The Book of Common Prayer. We can rediscover the true meaning of the Marriage Service and of its underlying principle, if we have a real understanding of the philosophical and natural basis upon which it rests. We want to know why our Lord spoke as he did concerning remarriage after divorce.

3. CONFUSION IN THE CHURCH.

When Canons 17 and 18 were adopted almost unanimously by the General Convention of 1946, they were widely hailed as "Miracle Canons". A feeling of relief swept over the Church, for it seemed that, at long last, a workable and happy solution for the very difficult and vexing question of the Church's discipline concerning marriage and divorce had been reached. This controversial issue had been debated in practically every General Convention since the year 1868.

In Philadelphia during the General Convention of 1946 the House of Bishops by 66 to 47 votes adopted an extremely liberal canon as introduced by the Commission on Holy Matrimony, which proposed to give to the Bishops wide discretionary powers concerning the remarriage of divorced persons. Almost im-

---

[25]*De libello repudii* (Homily on I Cor. vii., 39, 40).

mediately, however, an amendment to this liberal canon was added, which tied down the exercise of this discretionary power to a specified list of impediments to marriage. After some discussion the whole matter was referred to a special committee of five Bishops. This Committee was composed of the following: Bishops Scarlett, Davis, Conkling, Penick, and Gravatt. The next day, this Committee brought in an unanimous report, which was unanimously adopted by the House of Bishops and sent on to the House of Deputies, where it received quick and overwhelming approval.[20]

I was present in the gallery of the House of Bishops when this Committee made its report. What amazed me was the rapidity with which this important piece of legislation was enacted. The time involved was hardly more than thirty minutes. When the House adjourned for lunch, I went up to one of our most outstanding Bishops and asked, "Bishop, what does this mean?" "Edward," the Bishop replied, "I don't know." Then seeing my look of perplexity, he added, "I think it is a compromise!"

One wishes that the Bishops had slept at least one night over Canon 18, Section 2 (b), and had discussed the ways in which they intended to administer it. Apparently, there was great haste as illustrated by the fact that the prohibition concerning the remarriage of divorced persons by ministers of this Church was omitted and had to be put back into the Canon, as Canon 17, Section 6, by the General Convention of 1949.

I was profoundly disturbed during the discussion in the House of Bishops in 1946 on this question to hear one Bishop, an ardent advocate for a very liberal canon, plead with his fellow Bishops in this manner: "Gentlemen, we have got to recognize human nature!" On the contrary, the Church has been commissioned by our Lord Jesus Christ to bring about the redemption

---

[20] *Journal of the General Convention*, 1946, p. 247 ff.

of human nature, not the recognition of its frailty by liberalizing the Church's interpretation of God's eternal and divine laws.

It is not surprising that shortly after the General Convention of 1946 the unified, catholic and historic voice of the American Episcopal Church disintegrated into a babel of voices giving various and directly contradictory interpretations of Canon 18, Section 2(b). Dr. Edgar L. Pennington of Mobile, Alabama, the late historiographer of the Church, wrote to me during the past year, and said: "We are really in a state of confusion on the subject; the Bishops do not seem to have any uniform interpretation of the law, and the clergymen are certainly not unanimous in their understanding or practice."

The General Convention of 1949[27] made no substantial changes in Canon 18, Section 2(b). The prohibition against clergymen officiating at the marriages of divorced persons was restored. (Canon 17, Section 6.) Also an amendment was added requiring couples, who wish to be married by this Church, to sign a preliminary statement, which expresses their conformity to the Church's teaching on Holy Matrimony. A few other clarifying changes were effected.

Serious attempts, however, were made to clear up the confusion. As one of the deputies, I offered one brief amendment to Canon 18, Section 2(b), viz: "to exist or to have existed *ab initio*" in order to make it clear beyond any reasonable doubt that this Canon should be administered only in accordance with the principle of nullity and not that of divorce.

Another amendment was also offered which would have rewritten Canons 17 and 18, so as to eliminate confusion regarding its underlying principle of the indissolubility of marriage, according to the historic use of the term.

This confusion is the direct result of the ambiguous language of Canon 18, Section 2(b); viz., "but when any of the facts

---

[27] See *Journal of the General Convention*, 1949, pp. 163-175, for the record concerning action on amendments, etc., outlined herein.

set forth in Canon 17, Section 2, (b), are shown to exist or to have existed, which manifestly establish that no marriage bond as the same is recognized by this Church exists, the same may be declared by proper authority." This language does not clearly state that the impediments must have actually and really been in existence *ab initio*. It does not definitely and distinctly tie down the application of this Canon to the doctrine of nullity, though it can be, and, in the light of the Prayer Book, should be interpreted in that way.

Furthermore, these words in Canon 18, Section 2(b), to the effect that marriage is "in intention lifelong" are also ambiguous and are of very doubtful conformity to the principle of indissolubility in the Prayer Book.

These amendments, *supra*, which sought to clarify the Church's position on the remarriage of divorced persons, were laid aside by the House of Deputies and the whole matter referred to a Joint Commission to Report Recommendations as to Amendments to Canons on Holy Matrimony.[28] Also an amendment which was adopted by the House of Bishops, apparently designed to render Canon 18, Section 2(b), more liberal than its words might justify, was rejected by the House of Deputies. Also a somewhat similar and very liberal amendment to this Canon, which was proposed by a majority of the Committee on Canons of the House of Deputies, was likewise rejected by the House of Deputies. This amendment proposed to add the following words to Canon 18, Section 2(b): "When any of the facts set forth in Canon 17, Section 2(b), are shown to exist . . . *'or, if in the opinion of the Bishop or Ecclesiastical Authority,*

---

[28] This Commission in its Report to the General Convention of 1952 recommended that no changes in the marriage canons be made at this time; that it be continued to study the adequacy of the present Canons and to act as a clearing house for the exchange of information as to procedures etc.; that it prepare "for summission to the next General Convention such editorial alterations in Canons 16, 17, and 18 as may be needed to correct infelicities of expression." This Report was adopted by the General Convention, which directed the Committees on Canons of the two Houses to assist the Commission in that work.

PRELIMINARY CONSIDERATIONS   19

the annulment or dissolution of such marriage bond was otherwise justifiable in the eyes of the Church,"* the Bishop or the Ecclesiastical Authority may give judgment accordingly." If this had passed both Houses of General Convention, it would have amounted to a full acceptance of the doctrine of absolute divorce.

The procedure concerning the amendment and adoption of canons in the House of Deputies is not what one would expect. So far as we know, there is no requirement that such a proposal should have two readings and thus pass the House at least twice. The liberal proposal of the Committee on Canons, *supra,* was presented without preliminary notice, and without mimeographed copies being placed in the hands of the deputies. Surely, it would seem that, with all the thousands of dollars expended on General Convention, the House of Deputies could afford enough stenographic help to have each day's journal of the Convention mimeographed and given to the deputies the first thing on the following day. Furthermore, no changes in our Canons, or additions thereto, should become the law of the Church, until each proposal shall have passed at least two readings of the House. If such a change passes the House once, it will probably pass very quickly the second time; such is normal legislative procedure in order to check or limit legislative ignorance and irresponsibility.

Bishop Conkling in a statement published soon after General Convention declared: "This General Convention would thus seem to reflect what is the general mind throughout the Church —that our present canons on marriage are the best we have had for many years, and we need to live and work under them to test them fully before making important changes."[20]

We find it difficult to agree with this statement. The de-

---
*Italics mine.
[20]*The Living Church,* October 10, 1949.

bate in the House of Deputies (1949) on this issue was the most heated discussion of the entire General Convention; this was certainly true of the proceedings in the Lower House. Newspaper correspondent Carolyn Anspacher, writing for the *San Francisco Chronicle*, Oct. 7, 1949, declared:

> A headlong clash between ultra-conservatives and liberals of the Protestant Episcopal Church was sidestepped late yesterday when the House of Deputies deferred major amendments in the marriage canons for another three years. The two factions met with considerable oratorical violence while considering the general subject of divorce as it pertains to members of the Church. . . . After a heated two-hour-long debate, the deputies decided to put the matter into the hands of a special commission for study. . . .

During this debate, one chancellor declared that an unofficial survey of the administration of the marriage canons has revealed the amazing fact that sixty per cent of our Bishops are interpreting this Canon on the basis of nullity; that is, they are refusing permission for remarriage after divorce unless the impediment actually existed at the time of the former marriage; whereas, forty per cent of our Bishops are interpreting these same Canons on the basis of absolute divorce (divorce *a vinculo matrimonii*); viz., that a marriage may be dissolved for causes, such as the impediments listed in Canon 17, Section 2(b), arising after the formation of a valid bond of matrimony. In support of this conclusion of the unofficial survey, *supra*, we quote the following statement made by the Committee on Canons of the House of Deputies which was attached to their proposal to amend Canon 18, Section 2(b), so as to recognize "the annulment or dissolution of such marriage bond" if, in the opinion of the Bishop, such "was otherwise justifiable in the eyes of the Church," (see *supra*):

The Committee believes that the resolution as revised more nearly conforms to the *divergent construction and application of this section of* Canon 18 *in the various Dioceses and Missionary Districts** since its revision by the General Convention of 1946.[30]

We are happy to add the following:

The House did not accept the report of the Committee.[31]

This state of confusion, however, is deplorable and demands that the basic issues involved in Canon 18, Section 2(b), be honestly re-examined and carefully studied. The Church can not face both ways at the same time on any principle so fundamental as the indissolubility of marriage.

The General Convention of 1946 was absorbed in the problems of reunion with the Presbyterian Church. In 1949, the General Convention spent most of its energy and time on the problems of clergy pensions, the expanded budget of the National Council, and the new program of Christian education. It would seem that one of the vital issues before the Church now is the all important institution of marriage with the resulting family relationships. The underlying principle of the family, which is the basic unit of our society and civilization, is the indissolubility of the bond of matrimony. It is only by a return to such a sound principle that the confusion existing in the Church can be cleared up.

All agree, we are sure, that the return to sound principle requires studying anew the mind of our blessed Lord and Saviour, Jesus Christ.

---

*Italics mine.
[30]*Journal of the General Convention* 1949, p. 173.
[31]*Idem*, p. 173.

CHAPTER II

THE MIND OF CHRIST ON MARRIAGE AND DIVORCE

1. The Reliability of the Sayings of Jesus concerning Marriage and Divorce
2. The New Testament Passages
3. Some Modern Viewpoints on the Mind of Christ
   a. The School of Divorce
   b. The School of Indissolubility

THE MIND OF CHRIST
ON MARRIAGE AND DIVORCE

THERE are a number of modern viewpoints on this problem in the American Episcopal Church and also in the Church of England. By modern, we refer to what may be described as twentieth century interpretations of our Lord's sayings on this subject.

Before discussing these opinions, let us make it absolutely clear that the sincerity of all is assumed. This is obvious from the fact that their positions are presented; as Dr. Cirlot has said: "Their sincerity is beyond question. If I had any doubt about it, it would be a waste of time to write this book."[1]

All of us, regardless of sharp differences of opinion, are agreed that the mind of Christ on this subject must be the criterion in determining the doctrine and discipline of the Church on the subject.

> It is the duty and the responsibility both of every instructed Christian, as well as of each branch of the Church, to decide as best they may, under the guidance of the Holy Ghost, what is the mind of Christ on this difficult and important subject.[2]

1. THE RELIABILITY OF THE SAYINGS OF JESUS CONCERNING MARRIAGE AND DIVORCE.

The teaching of our Lord on this subject is as reliably authenticated as anything he ever taught. What he said was recorded or reflected first in the Epistles of St. Paul, which were written before the Gospels. Then it appeared in St. Mark's Gospel, published in Rome probably about the year 65 A.D. St.

---
[1] *Christ and Divorce*, Preface, p. i.
[2] MacMillan, *op. cit.*, p. 38.

Luke's Gospel and St. Matthew's Gospel, with variations as to the form of this teaching but not as to its substance, are in accord with St. Mark's Gospel, except possibly for the famous Matthean Exception.

The substance of the Gospels existed in the form of an oral or only partially recorded tradition after the crucifixion of Christ until the Epistles of St. Paul were written and St. Mark's Gospel appeared. It is entirely possible that the sayings of Jesus and other information or narratives were written down during our Lord's ministry or immediately after his death. A few years after the appearance of St. Mark's Gospel (65—70 A.D.), St. Luke's Gospel came into existence, probably during the decade 70-80 A.D. The date of St. Matthew's Gospel is placed during the period 80-100 A.D.

We have good reasons to believe that St. Matthew's Gospel, in its present form, was not written by the Apostle Matthew, but was compiled by a later hand. The evidence is also convincing that the compiler of St. Matthew's Gospel and St. Luke, St. Paul's companion missionary, both used the oldest Gospel: i.e., St. Mark's.

There is, however, some material which is peculiar to St. Matthew's Gospel, this being called "M"; and some which is peculiar to St. Luke's Gospel, which source is called "L". The former is composed of "Matthean additions" and is not strictly a source because the compiler of this Gospel only had access to the tradition of the Palestinian Church in addition to Mark and Q. The latter, however, was based on St. Luke's personal investigations. In fact, it has been suggested by Streeter that there was first in existence "Proto-Luke" composed of Q and L. Then St. Luke used Mark's Gospel to complete his Gospel as we now have it, using these three sources: i.e., Mark, Q and L.[3] Also there is a substantial amount of non-Markan material

---

[3] Ency. Brit. Vol. 3, p. 523.

used by both Matthew and Luke, which scholars have named "Q" (from the German *Quelle,* which means source).

> There is almost universal agreement among scholars that Q is a very early document originating in one of the earliest periods of the Church's history. Its contents suggest that it was a kind of handbook of Apologetic for Christian teachers ... there is almost universal agreement among scholars that Q is an earlier document than St. Mark's Gospel. In fact, there seems to be reason for supposing that St. Mark had some knowledge (perhaps only a recollection of some of the contents) of Q. ... Indeed, when one considers the enormous preponderance of sayings over deeds in Q and the corresponding preponderance of deeds over sayings in Mark, one may reasonably speculate that St. Mark wrote not only with a recollection of Q, but actually to supplement it.[4]

Because Papias, who was Bishop of Hierapolis in Asia Minor about 140 A.D., said that "Matthew in the Hebrew tongue wrote down the oracles[5] (logia), and every man interpreted them as he was able" there has been much speculation to the effect that possibly these logia can be identified as Q, but "the Matthaean authorship of Q is not more than a reasonable possibility."[6] Some think it safer to say only that Q is composed of non-Markan material in St. Matthew's and St. Luke's Gospels.

The primary sources, therefore, for our Lord's sayings on marriage and divorce and other questions, are St. Mark's Gospel, Q, M and L.

Further proof of the authentic nature of the logia of Jesus is derived from the fact that the Catholic and Apostolic Church, from the earliest times, has been the faithful custodian of these early records.

[4]Gore's *Commentary* pp. 38 and 39.
[5]Logia of Jesus.
[6]Gore's *Commentary* p. 39.

The evidence which we have is the testimony of eyewitnesses. St. Mark was St. Paul's fellow labourer and most probably the interpreter for St. Peter (Acts 12:12, 25; 13:5, 13; 15:37, 39; Col. 4:10; Philemon 24; I Peter 5:13; 2 Tim. 4:11). His home was a center of apostolic activity (Acts 12:12). It may have been the house in which the Last Supper was held.[7]

St. Luke, the "beloved physician" and fellow traveler of the great apostle, St. Paul, made a careful investigation into all that Jesus said and did and reported the results of his interviews with eyewitnesses in his wonderful Gospel of which he is considered to be the author according to an early and reliable tradition.

If St. Matthew was the author of Q, we have again the direct evidence of a reliable eyewitness and hearer of the logion on marriage and divorce.

St. Paul's statements concerning the teaching of Christ on marriage and divorce are to be found in his Epistles to the Corinthians, Romans, and Ephesians. There is no serious question concerning his authorship of I and II Corinthians and Romans.[8] The Pauline authenticity of "Ephesians" has been questioned by some competent scholars but there seems to be no compelling reason to be swayed by such opinion.[9] There is certainly no doubt about St. Paul's reliable interpretation of the mind of our Lord on this and other subjects.

It is possible for one to say that our Lord did not *mean* what he said about marriage and divorce but it seems very foolish indeed to take the position that he did not *say* in substance what he is reported to have said according to the first three Gospels.

It is unnecessary to go any further into the technical details of the sources of the Gospels. What has been set forth ought to be sufficient to enable the laity to appreciate the authentic

---

[7] Gore's *Commentary* p. 43.
[8] See Gore's *Commentary*.
[9] See Gore's and Dummelow's Commentaries.

nature of the logia of Jesus among which none enjoys greater reliability than his sayings on the remarriage of divorced persons. (The authenticity of the Matthean Exception will be considered hereinafter.)

We ought to bear in mind the fact that St. Mark's Gospel was written for the Gentiles, and for a world in which, according to Roman law, a woman could divorce her husband. On the other hand, St. Matthew's Gospel was compiled for the Jewish world, and is coloured with Jewish thought.

2. THE NEW TESTAMENT PASSAGES.[10]

The ultimate source of authority in our Church on this and other problems of faith and conduct is the Bible.

> Here we have, then, a continual Court of Appeal. The living Church must do the teaching in every generation, but the written Book must continually test and correct the teaching. The Church must teach, but the Bible must prove. 'Do not believe what I say simply,' says an old Church teacher and Bishop, Cyril of Jerusalem, in his catechetical lectures, 'unless you find proof of it in the Holy Scriptures'. Here is the ideal—the Bishop or Church teaching; the Bible, continually in the hands of all Church people, keeping the teaching pure.[11]

For the convenience of the reader we will quote the most important passages on marriage and divorce in the New Testament, especially those which deal with the indissolubility of marriage.

a. *The Epistles of St. Paul*

These, you will remember, were written before the Gospels and can be dated in a general way by placing them in the decade 50-60 A.D.

(1) Romans 7:1-3

---

[10] From the King James Version.
[11] Charles Gore, *The Creed of the Christian*, p. 59.

1. Know ye not, brethren, (for I speak to them that know the law,) how that the law hath dominion over a man as long as he liveth?

2. For the woman which hath an husband is bound by the law to her husband so long as he liveth; but if the husband be dead, she is loosed from the law of her husband.

3. So then if, while her husband liveth, she be married to another man, she shall be called an adulteress: but if her husband be dead, she is free from the law; so that she is no adulteress. though she be married to another man.

(2) I Cor. 7

1. Now concerning the thing whereof ye wrote unto me . . .

10. And unto the married I command, *yet not I, but the Lord,* Let not the wife depart from her husband:

11. But and if she depart, let her remain unmarried, or be reconciled to her husband: and let not the husband put away his wife.

12. But to the rest speak I, not the Lord; If any brother hath a wife that believeth not, and she be pleased to dwell with him, let him not put her away.

13. And the woman which hath an husband that believeth not, and if he be pleased to dwell with her, let her not leave him.

14. For the unbelieving husband is sanctified by the wife, and the unbelieving wife is sanctified by the husband: else were your children unclean; but now are they holy.

15. But if the unbelieving depart, let him depart. A brother or a sister is not under bondage in such cases: but God hath called us to peace. . . .

39. The wife is bound by the law as long as her husband liveth; but if her husband be dead, she is at liberty to be married to whom she will; only in the Lord.

(3) Ephesians 5

31. For this cause shall a man leave his father and mother,

and shall be joined unto his wife, and they two shall be one flesh.

32. This is a great mystery: but I speak concerning Christ and the church.

b. *The Gospels*

(1) St. Mark 10

2. And the Pharisees came to him, and asked him, Is it lawful for a man to put away his wife? tempting him.

3. And he answered and said unto them, What did Moses command you?

4. And they said, Moses suffered to write a bill of divorcement, and to put her away.

5. And Jesus answered and said unto them, For the hardness of your heart he wrote you this precept.

6. But from the beginning of the creation God made them male and female.

7. For this cause shall a man leave his father and mother, and cleave to his wife;

8. And they twain shall be one flesh: so then they are no more twain, but one flesh.

9. What therefore God hath joined together, let not man put asunder.

10. And in the house his disciples asked him again of the same matter.

11. And he saith unto them, Whosoever shall put away his wife, and marry another, committeth adultery against her.

12. And if a woman shall put away her husband, and be married to another, she committeth adultery.

(2) St. Luke 16

18. Whosoever putteth away his wife, and marrieth another, committeth adultery: and whosoever marrieth her that is put away from her husband committeth adultery.

(3) St. Matthew 5

31. It hath been said, Whosoever shall put away his wife, let him give her a writing of divorcement:

32. But I say unto you, That whosoever shall put away his wife, saving for the cause of fornication, causeth her to commit adultery: and whosoever shall marry her that is divorced committeth adultery.

St. Matthew 19

3. The Pharisees also came unto him, tempting him, and saying unto him, Is it lawful for a man to put away his wife for every cause?

4. And he answered and said unto them, Have ye not read, that he which made them at the beginning made them male and female,

5. And said, For this cause shall a man leave father and mother, and shall cleave to his wife: and they twain shall be one flesh?

6. Wherefore they are no more twain, but one flesh. What therefore God hath joined together, let not man put asunder.

7. They say unto him, Why did Moses then command to give a writing of divorcement and to put her away?

8. He saith unto them, Moses because of the hardness of your hearts suffered you to put away your wives: but from the beginning it was not so.

9. And I say unto you, Whosoever shall put away his wife, except it be for fornication, and shall marry another, committeth adultery: and whoso marrieth her which is put away doth commit adultery.

10. His disciples say unto him, If the case of the man be so with his wife, it is not good to marry.

11. But he said unto them, All men cannot receive this saying, save they to whom it is given.

12. For there are some eunuchs, which were so born from their mother's womb: and there are some eunuchs which were

made eunuchs of men: and there be eunuchs, which have made themselves eunuchs for the kingdom of heaven's sake. He that is able to receive it, let him receive it.

Other references to marriage in the New Testament are: Mt. 22:29, 30; Mk. 12:24, 25; Lk. 20:34-36; 2 Cor. 6:14-18; Col. 3:18-19; I Tim. 3:2-4, 12; I Tim. 4:1-5; Heb. 13:4; I Peter 3:1-7. These passages do not directly involve the question of the remarriage of divorced persons, but they are of interest.

The following passage from Deut. 24 is the most important one in the Old Testament:

1. When a man hath taken a wife, and married her, and it come to pass that she find no favour in his eyes, because he hath found some uncleanness in her: then let him write her a bill of divorcement, and give it in her hand, and send her out of his house.

2. And when she is departed out of his house, she may go and be another man's wife.

The dispute among the Jewish rabbis revolved around the question of what constituted "some uncleanness." No one in Israel had even dreamt of our Lord's uncompromising position concerning the absolute indestructibility of the bond of matrimony. It was simply a question of whether or not it was lawful for a man to send his wife out of his house with his personal writing of divorcement only for unchastity or for every cause.

Opinion was divided between the two Schools of Shammai and Hillel. The former taught that divorce should be allowed only for the one cause of "uncleanness", probably adultery. They believed that "the putting away of a wife is odious."[12] This School seemed to be more in line with the teaching of the prophet Malachi: "Let none deal treacherously against the wife of his youth. For the Lord, the God of Israel, saith that he hateth putting away."[13]

---

[12]Dummelow's *Commentary* p. 688.
[13]2:15, 16.

The School of Hillel taught that divorce should be permitted for every cause, i.e., "If the wife cook her husband's food ill, by over-salting or over-roasting it, she is to be put away".[14]

The Matthean form of the opening question put to our Lord, rather than the Markan, is more correct, i.e.: "Is it lawful for a man to put away his wife for *every cause?*" In his reply, our Lord very obviously did not agree with either Shammai or Hillel. There is no other way to explain the surprise and amazement of his disciples; a fact which is devastating to the Matthean Exception as a ground for the remarriage of the innocent party in a divorce for adultery.

MacMillan says: "As a matter of law the opinion of the school of Hillel prevailed".[15]

The problems presented by the passages from the New Testament, *supra,* are:

(1) Did our Lord mean by his words that a valid bond of marriage is absolutely indissoluble and indestructible as a fact in the order of nature; or did he intend his statement as an unique piece of legislation on his part; or did he wish to convey the thought that the indissolubility of marriage is only an ideal or a counsel of perfection toward which his disciples should strive?

(2) Did he mean that a valid bond of marriage cannot be dissolved regardless of extremely sad, difficult, hard, and unfortunate cases?

(3) Which form of his teaching on this subject is the most reliable from the standpoint of historicity—the Matthean, the Markan or the Lukan form? If all of these forms teach the absolute indissolubility of marriage in substance, are these variations in form of a serious nature?

(4) Is the Matthean Exception genuine? If so, is it to be

---

[14]Dummelow's *Commentary* p. 688.
[15]*Op. cit.,* p. 20. Cf. Gore's *Commentary, Infra,* p. 53.

interpreted as giving only the right of separation or divorce *a mensa et thoro*?

(5) If he did mean that remarriage after divorce constitutes a life of habitual adultery, can one be forgiven for a former marital failure, due primarily or partially to his own selfishness, relieved of his sacred vows of matrimony before God's altar and permitted to enter into a new marriage?

(6) Can our Lord's saying on marriage and divorce be limited to the Jewish thinking of the first Century concerning adultery?

According to the Jewish standards of that day, a married man would not have been considered guilty of adultery, if he had intercourse with an unmarried woman. If his relations, however, were with a married woman, he would have been charged with the crime. Also under Jewish law a married woman could not divorce her husband. This being so, did our Lord mean only that a man who divorces his wife causes her to commit adultery since, being without a home, she has no other way to live? Are his words so un-Jewish in form that their historicity can be legitimately attacked?

"Except it be for fornication": does this refer to the fact that if she is already an adulteress, then a bill of divorcement will not cause her to become one?

Some of the efforts to answer these questions will be set forth in the following section.

3. Some Modern Viewpoints on the Mind of Christ.

It is difficult to know how one should classify the two schools of thought on this subject in our Church. There can be no doubt, in view of the sharp differences of opinion and practice among our Bishops, that two such schools do exist. We have considered the following classifications:

    Liberalism vs Conservatism
    Evangelicalism vs Anglo-Catholicism
    High Church vs Low Church

Such categories, however, do not fit the facts, for there are low and liberal Churchmen who are staunch advocates of the absolute indissolubility of marriage, and, on the other hand, there are Anglo-Catholics and conservative Churchmen who are willing to stretch the doctrine of nullity to the point where it is really the same thing as divorce *a vinculo matrimonii*.

Furthermore, it is requisite and expedient for all Churchmen to gravitate more and more away from extreme positions, avoiding as much as possible party labels and classifications, especially when the essential principles of the Catholic faith, according to the teaching of the Book of Common Prayer, are concerned.

Thus, any essential principle of the doctrine and discipline of Christ should be re-examined from the viewpoint of how "this Church hath received the same". (Prayer Book p. 542.) We need to study the mind of Christ more as Churchmen and less as partisans.

We are nearer the truth, therefore, if we classify the two schools of thought and practice on this subject as *The School of Divorce* and *The School of Indissolubility*.

a. *The School of Divorce*

Some or all of those listed below under this category will probably protest because they are made to appear as approving of divorce. We reassure anyone that all that is meant is that they accept the principle of divorce *a vinculo matrimonii*, i.e., that in certain difficult cases the bond of marriage can be dissolved for causes arising after the formation of such a bond.

Of course, they would all agree, we are sure, that the breakup of a marriage in the divorce courts is a tragic affair; a real departure from the ideal of Christ, and a failure in Christian living. They do believe, however, that, for a cause arising after marriage, a valid bond of marriage can be dissolved. In other words, they accept in one way or another the principle of divorce *a vinculo matrimonii,* and the inevitable corollary, i.e., that the remarriage of divorced persons does not constitute adultery in the eyes of God. Examples of this viewpoint follow:

(1) Burton Scott Easton, S.T.D., Ph.D., before his death Professor of New Testament Literature and Interpretation, General Theological Seminary.

His view is set forth in an article entitled "Divorce and The New Testament",[16] which was reprinted for The Joint Commission on Marriage and Divorce of the General Convention together with a letter, dated March 18, 1940, from Bishop Gardner of New Jersey to Bishop Page of Michigan in which the Bishop of New Jersey said:

> I am very happy that the Commission has seen fit to print and distribute this interesting paper by Dr. Easton. It has already proved itself of value to the clergy of the Diocese of New Jersey, to whom I have had the pleasure of reading it.... I am certain that this should be in the hands of all who are to participate in the General Convention in October.

Dr. Easton, in a novel approach to the mind of Christ, strikes at the very authenticity of the saying of Jesus that remarriage after divorce is adultery. His position is initiated with the idea that the marriage ceremony and the bill of divorcement among the Jews and the Romans were personal acts and were not dealt with by public officials. He also reminds us that adultery in the Jewish world was always an offense by a married woman against her husband; a man being guilty of it only if he committed adultery with another man's wife.

He considers that our Lord in Mark 10:2-9, which ends with the words—"What therefore God hath joined together, let not man put asunder"—sets forth "the divine ideal" (Gen. 2:24), and that permission to grant a personal bill of divorcement, ac-

---
[16] *Anglican Theological Review,* Vol. XXII, April, 1940.

cording to Mosaic law, was a concession to men because of their hardheartedness to the will of God. We quote Dr. Easton at length because his views have had a widespread influence upon the members of the Joint Commissions on Holy Matrimony and many others throughout the Church:

> The primary passage containing Christ's teaching on divorce is Mark 10:2-9, which records a discussion in strict rabbinic style. . . . Christ replies that this concession by Moses is due to men's hardheartedness; the same Moses stated the divine ideal in Genesis 2:24. Therefore, since it is the ideal, not the concession, that men ought to follow, the conclusion is clear: 'What God hath joined together, let not man put asunder'.
>
> To this public discussion Mark appends a 'private' explanation given to the disciples. Such explanations Gospel students have learned to view with some suspicion; in at least three cases in the Second Gospel (4:10 ff; 7:17 ff; 13:3 ff) they contain not the actual words of Christ but very *early interpretations** of the Church. And in the case of Mark 10:10-12 the interpretative character is unmistakable. The second clause, 'If a woman shall put away her husband and marry another, she committeth adultery' states something impossible in Palestine. . . . And in the first clause, 'Whosoever shall put away his wife and marry another, committeth adultery against her', 'adultery' appears in a sense that no Jew would use or understand. . . .
>
> Abstractly, of course, it would be conceivable that it was Christ Himself who first used 'adultery' in this new sense and so raised woman to man's plane. . . . But against this supposition the evidence of the First Gospel is decisive, for in Matthew 5:31-32 great pains are taken to avoid this foreign sense of the word. . . . Here everything is strictly Jewish. There is no question of the first husband's adultery, if he remarry, for no Jew would so describe his conduct. He is, however, responsible for his wife's sin; the

---
*Italics mine.

passage taking for granted that she will either remarry or fall into a life of shame. . . .

But in one case the first husband cannot be said to make her an adulteress if he put her away, and that is if by her own act she has already made herself one while still married to him. Consequently, the famous 'exceptional clause' is not a gloss but essential to the completeness of statement; its presence in Mt. 5:32 gives the verse Rabbinic preciseness. This very preciseness, however, tells strongly against it as an authentic statement of Christ. . . . If, however, Christ Himself had given 'adultery' its Markan-Lukan definition, Matthew would not have had recourse to so roundabout a device but would have cited the Lord's words directly.

Dr. Easton then adds that Mt. 19:9, according to some ancient authorities, should read exactly as Mt. 5:32, and says:

What Christ actually taught, then, was: a man and his wife 'are no longer two, but one flesh; what, therefore, God has joined together, let not man put asunder'. This and no more; the other verses cited above are very early Christian rules deduced from this primary saying. . . .

It was Christ's manner simply to state a principle in its most extreme form, without indicating in anyway how His statement is to be applied . . . when Christ uttered the saying, He uttered it for the consciences of individuals. . . . Each man must decide his own case . . . when to take an oath, not to turn the other cheek. . . . To erect any of Christ's principles into a law that will take into account all the possible exceptions and yet do full justice to the moral rigor demanded is impossible.

Dr. H. C. Robbins, in his article, "The Teaching of Christ concerning Marriage",[17] interprets Dr. Easton's position in these words:

---

[17]From the booklet of The Joint Commission of the General Convention (1937) entitled: "An Introduction to the Study of Canon 41." See also *The Southern Churchman*, December 26. 1936.

Consequently, the directions about divorce in Christ's teaching are as immediately personal as the directions about turning the other cheek. Christ was not discussing what is the best marriage law for a state or even a church: He was telling how conscientious individuals ought to act.

(2) Dr. Frederick C. Grant, Union Theological Seminary.

His views were published in an article on "The Mind of Christ on Marriage", in pamphlet form, by the Joint Commission on Holy Matrimony (1946).[18]

The essence of his position in this article is that the saying of our Lord on the principle of indissolubility is authentic, regardless of the various forms in which it appears in Matthew, Mark, and Luke, but that it is a prophetic condemnation and "a counsel of perfection"; it is not legislation by our Lord.

He recognizes that Mark 10:12 is a Markan application of this teaching to Roman life, since a Jewish woman could not divorce her husband as a Roman woman could, but he describes it as "nevertheless, a quite legitimate corollary".

He also emphasizes the importance of Mark's Gospel as the primary source. Some scholars think that Mt. 5:31-32 came from Q, which was used by Matthew, Luke, and also Mark. "But I cannot resist the suspicion", continues Dr. Grant, "that 5:32 is also based on Mark, or on a form of the saying that likewise underlies Mark; the introduction to the saying, in verse 31, is strongly reminiscent of the dialogue with the Pharisees in Mk. 10:2-9".

Dr. Grant also feels that Luke 16:18, an apparent abrupt intrusion into the text, reflects the influence of Mt. 5:32, and, therefore, "does not come from 'Q', but from some other source, perhaps from the later source 'M'."

Dr. Grant then says:

---

[18]*Infra.* p. 129. See also *Five Essays on Marriage* by B. S. Easton et al., Chapter III.

If this analysis is correct, then the saying is not one of those found in both Mark and 'Q', but is primarily Markan; but—and this is even more important, and is an inescapable inference from a study of the form of the saying—it is so old a saying, so deeply imbedded in the tradition of Jesus' words . . . that it can only be viewed as one of the most incontestable and unquestionable sayings attributed to our Lord in all the evangelic literature.

This scholar does not recognize the authenticity of the Matthean Exception, saying:

> . . . the Matthean form of the saying does not state that it is 'lawful' for a man to put away his wife for the one cause, viz., that she was not a virgin when he married her, but only that in such a case (so it is implied) he does not 'make' her an adulteress. Such a statement of the lawfulness of divorce in some cases, would have been answering the Pharisees of Mark 10 in the way they hoped to be answered! . . . It was added, as many modern commentators and exegetes believe, during the course of the handing down of Christ's teaching by oral tradition.

Dr. Grant also disagrees with the idea that the phrase in Mt. 5:32 i.e., "causes her to commit adultery" is "the original form of the saying, and that the simple 'commits adultery,' as in Matt. 19:9, Mk. 10:11, and Lk. 16:18, is a secondary form."

This scholar's interpretation of the authentic logion, as he thinks the Church should apply the same, is expressed in the following words:

> There is no use trying to soften Jesus' prophetic announcements on this subject. They were not enunciated as principles of law but as proclamations of the 'pure will of God' . . . they were not intended to form a section in a legal code. . . . If one is to live in accordance with the pure will of God, this is what he must do. . . . Stated in theological terms, Jesus' proclamation is a 'counsel of per-

fection,' like that addressed to the rich man: 'If thou wouldest be perfect, etc.' . . . a rule of life for those who are committed to a complete obedience to the will of God. . . .

Dr. Grant in a former article entitled "The Proposed Marriage Canon"[19] had accepted Dr. Easton's position that the saying about remarriage after divorce being adultery is not authentic but merely an early interpretation or rule made by the Church.

In this article, Dr. Grant interprets Mark 10:8-9 "as setting forth the ideal of marriage . . . along with this is the reformulation[20] of Jesus' teaching as rules governing the Church." In another part of this article this author speaks of Mark 10:11-12 and also Luke 16:18, which refer to remarriage after divorce as a life of adultery, as "the formulation of our Lord's teaching as law under Gentile conditions." He also interprets Matthew 5:32 as the formulation of the saying "under Jewish conditions". This scholar then concludes: "Such formulations[21] should be recognized for what they are: incipient Canon law, rather than accurate records of Jesus' teaching". Apparently, Dr. Grant now holds the position set forth above in his article "The Mind of Christ on Marriage."

(3) Dr. Bayard H. Jones, School of Theology, University of the South, Sewanee, Tennessee.

His position is to be found in an article entitled "Marriage and Divorce".[22]

After stating that marriage is a permanent relationship "grounded in the nature of human life", he presents Jewish thought and practice on this subject during the lifetime of Jesus, saying: "It is against this Jewish background that we must in-

---

[19] *The Anglican Theological Review*, Vol. XXII, pp. 169-181, July, 1940.
[20] That is to say, in Mark 10:11-12.
[21] The reference is to Mk. 10:11-12; Lk. 16:18; Mt. 5:32.
[22] Reprinted from the *Anglican Theological Review*. Vol. XXIV, January 1942.

terpret our Lord's teaching". He states that "polygamy was still perfectly legal among the Jews; though its practice had become somewhat rare, from the impoverishment of the nation from many wars. To all appearances this continued to be the case among Christians in Apostolic times."

He interprets I Tim. 3:2 "a bishop" or "a deacon" (I Tim. 3:12) "should be the husband of one wife" as simply meaning that "any man consecrating himself to the service of the Church ought to be freed from multiplied previous obligations. Only as Monogamy came to be enforced on every member of the Church, was this expression understood as prohibiting digamy as well as bigamy to the church officers."

Dr. Jones points out that there are four statements on this problem, i.e., Mt. 5:31, 32; Lk. 16:18; Mk. 10:2-9; Mt. 19:3-9; he says that "three of the four statements are not even possible in our Lord's mouth in a Jewish setting; although we can see well enough how the tradition of what he did say could have developed into its present forms in the understanding of Gentile Christians. . . ."

Then, assuming the basic and primary nature of the Markan account, Dr. Jones attacks the historicity of the second half of the saying, i.e., "And if a woman shall put away her husband and be married to another, she committeth adultery."[23]

"Now the second statement", Dr. Jones continues, "in v. 12, simply could not have been said by our Lord to Jews. We have seen that no Jewish woman had any right whatever to divorce her husband. There could have been no point in saying what she would be if she could and did, when as a matter of fact she could not. Such an expression, however, might well enough have originated in St. Peter's audience at Rome, who were habituated to the equal right of men and women under Roman divorce law. To them, it might have seemed an obvious formulation of the

---
[23]Mk. 10:12.

new moral rights of womankind, which they were quite correct in understanding our Lord to assert."

Dr. Jones feels, therefore, that Mark 10:12 should be considered as a Gentile gloss and not as authentic. Consequently, the second clause of this logion in Mt. 5:32 and 19:9 and in Luke 16:18 should also be looked upon as unauthentic inasmuch as they are dependent upon Mark 10:12.

He thinks that Mark 10:11 "remains as a general condemnation of the arbitrary brutality of the Jewish permission to a man to get rid of his wife at his own will . . . what Malachi called 'treachery', Jesus stigmatizes bluntly by the name of a capital crime—Adultery. In so doing, our Lord was using sweeping prophetic language, rather than legally exact language. . . . Our Lord's condemnation of the inhumanities of Jewish divorce is in no wise offered as new legislation."

Dr. Jones' whole position rests on two premises: (a) the unhistorical nature of Mark 10:12, (b) and the idea that polygamy was permitted among the early Christians because it was the accepted practice of the Jews. If the second clause of the logion is unhistorical, then in the first clause Jesus was not using the word "adultery" legally but as a condemnation of Jewish brutality. Jesus could not have been using the word "adultery" in the legally exact sense in the first clause of the logion because it was not adultery for a Jew to marry another and have two wives at the same time.

As to the Matthean Exception, Dr. Jones asserts that "no MS. throws the slightest doubt on the authenticity of the Exception." St. Mark, he thinks, was in error in omitting the Exception and "missed the essential point on which the whole incident turned. I believe that the version in Matt. 19:9 represents an independent and more correct tradition". But he thinks that the "adultery" signifies "undisclosed pre-marital unchastity."

Dr. Jones feels that "Monogamy is a requirement of ecclesiastical rather than Scriptural origin", and being so, it is one concerning which the Church can grant dispensations.

In the light of these views and also of his statement in the concluding part of this article about the Church having a canon which should forbid our clergy to marry divorced persons, his position as to what kind of a doctrine we ought to have is not altogether clear. Apparently, he wants the Church "to enact a simple clearcut stand of forbidding the clergy to take any part whatever in the contraction or the benediction of marriages which the Church's basic principles do not permit it to approve." Probably, he would base this upon the ecclesiastical authority of the Church and not on the belief that our Lord announced the absolute indissolubility of marriage.

(4) The Rev. Walter H. Stowe, S.T.D.

According to Dr. Cirlot (p. 148) Dr. Stowe presented his views in *The Living Church*, October 24, 1942, in which article he speaks of two divergent positions which are to be found among the Catholic and Apostolic Churches. He defines these as the Roman and the Orthodox positions and concludes that there is "*no such thing nowadays as the Catholic doctrine concerning divorce.*"*[24] Either position can be taken as being a Catholic view, since both positions have received wide official acceptance in the Catholic Branches of the Church.

Hereinafter this position is considered. The idea, however, that other Catholic Churches have made provision for the remarriage of divorced persons has had a widespread influence on the American Episcopal Church.

(5) The Rt. Rev. Cameron J. Davis, D.D., late Bishop of Western New York.

Speaking to the Convention of his Diocese, January 28, 1946, Bishop Davis, after urging a "more realistic" attitude toward the remarriage of divorced persons, declared that "in many cases

---

*Italics mine.
[24]Cirlot, *op. cit.*, p. 148.

it is a greater sin against God and society for couples to stay together than to separate. . . . Remarriage in the Episcopal Church of persons whose previous marriages have been dissolved should be decided according to the individual merits of the case. A blanket law in the field of human relations is directly contrary to the mind of Christ. I have seen many cases where it seemed that our Lord, Himself, would permit a remarriage . . . and have had to refuse to marry those people because our Church canon recognizes only nine or ten grounds of annulment and one of divorce.[25] A God-made marriage is and should be indissoluble. That is Christ's teaching. Such a marriage can not be terminated. But most marital failures were never true marriages in the Christian sense. The couples were not free and competent to make a Christian marriage or there were physical and *mental impediments that became apparent later.*"*[26]

In the Report of the Special Committee of the House of Bishops on Procedure under Marriage Legislation to the General Convention of 1949, which was signed by Bishop Davis and by Bishop Tucker of Ohio, it is admitted that two divergent interpretations are permissible. This Report says:

> Some of the Bishops are troubled by what they believe to be an ambiguity in the phrase occurring in Canon 18, Section 2(b) 'But when any of the facts set forth in Canon 17, Section 2(b) are shown to exist or to have existed,' . . . But as a matter of fact there is no ambiguity here. The Canon recognizes two points of view as legitimate: one, that if one or more of the impediments existed before marriage, no marital bond was created; the other, that if one of the impediments arises after marriage, the marital bond is broken. It is well known that in two other branches of the Catholic Church, the one holds that only when

---

[25]Before 1946 the Canon allowed the remarriage of the innocent party in a divorce for adultery.

*Italics mine.

[26]*The Witness*, February 7, 1946.

causes have existed before marriage, which make the marriage null and void, can a second marriage be solemnized; the other, that certain causes arising after marriage may dissolve the marriage bond. The Anglican Communion[27] has heretofore held to the latter although it has recognized only one cause, namely, physical adultery, as sufficient to break the bond. Our own branch of the Anglican Communion in its former discipline recognized, as does the present Canon, both the doctrine of nullity and of divorce.[28] Our present Canon differs from the previous one only in its recognition that the same causes which nullify a marriage can also break the marital bond if they appear after marriage, and in that it does not specify adultery . . . a Bishop who holds that causes arising after marriage can dissolve the bond is permitted to give judgment accordingly within the limits of the general causes listed in the previous Canon as impediments.[29]

Bishop Gardner of New Jersey dissented, "affirming that only one point of view, that of the Doctrine of Nullity, should be in the Canon."[30]

(6) The Rt. Rev. W. E. Conkling, D.D., Bishop of Chicago.

One hesitates to classify Bishop Conkling as a member of the School of Divorce, but apparently it must be done on the ground that he has publicly favored the doctrine of extended nullity and also his remarks have indicated tacit consent to the existence in the Church of divergent interpretations of Canon 18, one of which actually follows the principle of absolute divorce.

If his position is misunderstood, it is hoped that he will let it be known that he has been placed in the wrong classification.

His views are important because he and Bishop Davis have

---

[27]Only the American Episcopal Church. See *infra.* p. 98.
[28]Only as a dispensation to the innocent party.
[29]Canon 17, Section 2(b). See *Journal of the General Convention,* 1949, p. 439-440.
[30]*Idem* p. 440.

been credited with having been primarily reponsible for the "Miracle Canons" of 1946.

Bishop Conkling's statements, in addition to the one on page 19, *supra,* are as follows:

> It will be seen that this new Canon 17[31] allows a certain range of interpretation. To many this will be its greatest weakness, allowing some bishops to be very strict and others perhaps very lax. . . . It is necessary that we see clearly that the principle of this Canon is no remarriage for causes which are not to be found *essentially exstent*[32] before the first or dissolved marriage, and which are contrary to the requirements and character of Christian marriage. *This canon is based on what might be called an extension of the principle of nullity.** It is based upon the principle that a valid marriage may not be dissolved by divorce but also that the Church may examine whether any marriage is valid or void according to the proper requirements for a Christian marriage and so declare it.
>
> The revision is not perfect, of course. We have not yet been able to produce the miracle of a perfect canon, nor perfect people to administer it flawlessly, but we now have marriage legislation which is a step toward that goal. We can give thanks that it holds fast to the true character of Christian marriage and that it attempts to provide a Christlike means of dealing with those who may have failed.[33]

At the meeting of the House of Bishops in Winston-Salem, North Carolina, November, 1947, he made another statement:

> Bishop Conkling of Chicago secured the floor, and said with warmth of feeling: 'The law as proposed and written is not the Canon I should prefer. *It contains in it what I*

---

[31] The reference is to Canon 18—See *Journal of the General Convention,* 1949.

[32] Note these words. They would seem to imply that the necessary impediment need not be developed but only potentially existent. All normal people possess "defects of personality" which are at all times essentially or potentially existent, yet still undeveloped.

*Italics mine.

[33] *The Living Church,* October 13, 1946.

call extended nullity. Just because we have had one or two notorious cases, and dirty linen has been washed in public,[34] I don't see why we should now proceed as the Chancellor of New York[35] or any chancellor directs. Thank God, I have no Chancellor. I should like to proceed, trying to interpret the Canon. I should like to keep our cases from the public press. (Applause.) *Interpreting the Canon means that there will be divergent rulings.*[*][36]

The affinity of thought about and approach to the interpretation and administration of Canon 18, Section 2(b), between Bishop Davis and Bishop Conkling seems fairly obvious from the following statement made by Bishop Davis before the conclusion of the discussion on this subject in this meeting of the House of Bishops (1947):

> While on my feet, I should like to pay tribute to the Bishop of Chicago for his lucid exposition. *The Canon does admit of two interpretations.*[*] We can act in one of two ways under it. We must follow our consciences.[37]

Bishop Conkling seems to take really the same position as that of Bishop Davis, when he speaks of "extended nullity" and causes "essentially existent" before the first or dissolved marriage. A thing is what it really is regardless of how freely you attach names to it. You can call a horse a cow or a donkey or even an angel, or whatever you wish, but, nevertheless, a horse is a horse and remains so.

The true historic principle of nullity means that no valid

---

[34]The denunciation in prophetic and scathing terms by the late Bishop Manning of the marriages of two clergymen of our Church to divorcees. (Dioceses of Lexington and Michigan.)

[35]During this discussion, Bishop Scarlett referred to the interpretation of the Chancellor of New York in these words: *"I object to having the causes before marriage the only causes of annulment."* (*The Living Church*, November 16, 1947.)

*Italics mine.

[36]*The Living Church*, November 16, 1947.

*Italics mine.

[37]*The Living Church*, November 16, 1947.

bond of marriage has *ever* existed due to the existence, actually and really, of a developed impediment before or at the very hour of the marriage. An undeveloped defect of personality or an undeveloped insanity at the time of marriage can not prevent the creation of a valid bond of matrimony. To accept the teaching that it does and to follow such an interpretation means the acceptance of the principle of divorce *a vinculo matrimonii*. If any Bishop is willing, as Bishop Conkling apparently is, to acquiesce in the permissibility of such an interpretation in the administration of Canon 18, Section 2(b), in our Church, such a Bishop can not be classified as one who is really loyal to the historic position of the Church on the indissolubility of marriage; nor can he be placed in the category of the School of Indissolubility.

> The theory of relief that best fits the Anglican position logically is that of annulment. That does not carry us very far, for in the definition of a policy governing human relations logic is often the least persuasive of factors. It is the conviction of the author of this paper that *the differences between those who favor an extension of the theory of annulment and those who favor a theory of divorce are largely verbal*,* but that does not make the differences less troublesome. Perhaps no quarrels are more bitter or irreconcilable than those that are merely verbal. (Dr. Frederick A. Pottle, Sterling Professor of English, Yale University, in his "Notes on the History of Marriage Legislation", printed for the Joint Commission on Holy Matrimony.)

b. *The School of Indissolubility*

This School includes those who believe that, according to the mind of Christ, a valid bond of marriage, once formed, no real impediments being in existence *ab initio*, can no more be dissolved than can the relationship of father and son, or that of

---

*Italics mine.

brother and sister. They take seriously the words: "And they twain shall be one flesh: so then they are no more twain, but one flesh. What therefore God hath joined together, let not man put asunder." (Mark 10:8, 9.) Consequently, all remarriage after divorce, unless the former marriage has been annulled, constitutes the grave sin of adultery, no matter how unfortunate the case might be or how many justifiable causes might have existed for separation or for a divorce *a mensa et thoro*.

(1) The Rt. Rev. Charles Gore, D.D.

In his book, *The Sermon on the Mount*, he takes the position that our Lord legislated on this subject:

> ... we notice, first of all, that our Lord proclaimed, as a prominent law of His new kingdom, the indissolubility of marriage. And for us as Christians it is perfectly plain that not all the parliaments or kings on earth can alter the law of our Lord. And if any ministers of Christ, or persons claiming to represent the Church of Christ, ever dare to let the commandment of men, in however high places, override the law of Christ, they are simply behaving in a way which brings them under the threat which our Lord so solemnly uttered: 'Whosoever shall be ashamed of me and of my words in this adulterous and sinful generation, the Son of Man also shall be ashamed of him, when he cometh in the glory of his Father with the holy angels.' Beyond all question, for the Church, and for all who desire to call themselves Christians, it is absolutely out of the question to regard those as married who, having been divorced, have been married again, contrary to the law of Christ, during the lifetime of their former partner. It is quite true that this indissolubility of marriage may press hardly upon individuals in exceptional cases. But so does every law which is for the welfare of mankind in general; and, press it hardly or softly, the words of our Lord are quite unmistakeable. He who refused to legislate on so many subjects legislated on this, and the simple question arises whether

we prefer the authority of Christ to any other authority whatever.[38]

Bishop Gore, however, recognized, in these earlier years (1896), the Matthean Exception probably because he believed that the principle of indissolubility was a promulgation of positive or revealed law by Jesus, who, at least in this one instance, acted as a lawgiver. Being such, it was proper for him to grant an exception to the innocent party. He says:

> But it is a law of interpretation that a command with a specific qualification is more precise than a general command without any specific qualification; and that the one where the qualification occurs must interpret the other where this qualification does not occur.[39]

Again on p. 218:

> He appears to be sanctioning in the case of an innocent and deeply aggrieved person a dispensation which violates the logic of the marriage tie on grounds of equity: but this carries with it no necessary consequence of a similar dispensation in favour of the chief offender.

In later years, however, Bishop Gore practically admitted that his position on the Matthean Exception was apparently untenable:

> It must be added that the critical conclusion that the exceptive clause in the first Gospel is an interpolation, which really alters the sense of our Lord's original utterance about marriage, and that his real teaching is that given in St. Mark's and St. Luke's Gospels, represents an impressive consensus of scholars from Germany, France, America, and our own country.[40]

---
[38] P. 69-70.
[39] P. 71.
[40] Bp. Gore's *The Question of Divorce* p. 23.

Bishop Gore's *Commentary*, in that portion on St. Matthew's Gospel, written by P. P. Levertoff and H. L. Goudge, states that the case against the Matthean Exception is overwhelming:

> ... almost all scholars are now agreed that the exceptive clauses here and in 5:32 were never spoken by Him. (i) No such exception is recognized in our other accounts of the Lord's teaching (Mk. 10:11, 12; Lk. 16:18; I Cor. 7:10, 11), and all are prior to Matthew. Where Matthew alters the meaning of his chief authority, Mark, his alteration hardly ever justifies itself, and here his exceptive clauses affect the very substance of the Lord's teaching. (ii) These exceptive clauses do not even harmonize with his own narrative. Throughout 5:17-48 our Lord is substituting the perfect standard of God for the standard recognized by the Jews of His day; but, if the exceptive clause is retained, our Lord's teaching is no higher than Shammai's. Here the exceptive clause seems to be inconsistent both with 4-8 and with 10. Why should the disciples be startled by the Shammaite teaching, probably the dominant view among contemporary Jews?[41]

(2) Canon T. A. Lacey of the Church of England.

Canon Lacey wrote a remarkable book on our problem, entitled *Marriage in Church and State* (1912, London, Publisher Robert Scott), which he dedicated to the Bishop of London, saying in this dedication: "To teach nothing but what the Catholic Church prescribes or allows is the purpose of your Lordship's obedient servant."

Canon Lacey takes the position that marriage, according to the mind of Christ, is a relationship in the order of nature, and, therefore, not only should not be but can not be dissolved, regardless of the stringency of circumstances surrounding hard cases. ". . . marriage," he says, "is a natural relation which can

---
[41] P. 174. The references are to chapters 5 and 19 of Mt.'s Gospel.

no more be dissolved by law than the relation of brother and sister."[42]

In a masterful manner he sets forth his interpretation of the mind of Christ in his first Chapter entitled, "Of marriage in the Order of Nature." Inasmuch as Bishop Kirk[43] has said that this book should be read by everyone who desires to become a master of the subject, it is well to quote copiously from passages dealing with the crux of our problem, i.e., the absolute indissolubility of a valid bond of marriage and the unlawfulness of marriage after divorce.

Canon Lacey begins by pointing out that human life is not stable like "the static condition" of most animals, because:

> The divine purpose is imperfectly fulfilled, by reason of the element of perversity which is perceptible in human nature, and which is theologically attributed to a falling away from original righteousness, or conformity to the creative idea. . . . There is not, as Aristotle thought, one fixed standard of civilization. . . . But none the less certain fundamental institutions can be made out, which are almost constant in human life, though subject to wide variations in detail; and in most cases an ideal can be ascertained, the practice falling short of it. . . . Such an instituition is marriage.
>
> Marriage is not an artificial regulation of human life, but a natural necessity. The continuance of the species requires a certain association of man and woman. For the mere begetting of children, a merely passing union would suffice; but more is required. The child requires close attention and long continued care. This is seen in the case of some other animals also, but nowhere in the same degree. For most of such cases, the ordinary provision of nature is a close association of the parents during the growth of the offspring, the female devoting herself almost entirely to them, the male guarding her and supplying her needs.

---

[42] *Op. cit.*, Preface p. x.
[43] See *Marriage and Divorce* p. ix.

This double parental instinct varies in strength; it is probably seen at its intensest in man. But here it is reinforced. Unlike other animals, man gives birth to fresh offspring while those already born are still entirely dependent on the parents. . . . The connexion of the parents, therefore, is indefinitely prolonged, extending even beyond the age of childbearing. . . . As a consequence of this prolonged intimacy there appears the singular phenomenon of human love, which touches on the one hand the ordinary sexual desire of the animal world, but extends on the other hand into an habitual affection from which the element of desire may be entirely eliminated. . . . In a word, the human species is naturally constituted in families.

Marriage is nothing else but this permanent connexion of man and woman for the purpose of producing and raising children. Being thus natural, it is divinely ordered.[44]

The reason why marriage is in the order of nature is that only in monogamy can the true ends of marriage be achieved, such as "mutual trustfulness and accommodation", so necessary between man and wife, and the needs of the family, which include the guardianship and the nurture of the children, and the adequate protection and support of their mother by their father. Thus, "the civilization which insists on monogamy is in the true order of human development".[45]

Canon Lacey's remarks on polygamy are most interesting:

. . . polygamy can be shown to militate actively against the well-being of the race, which must be assumed as a true object of the natural order. It is found in practice to make for less fecundity. . . . The gravest objection, however, is that under normal conditions polygamy condemns a proportion of one sex to sterility, and to the moral evils flowing from the frustration of natural instincts. . . .

Polygamy, whether in its usual form or in the rarer form

---

[44]*Op. cit.*, pp. 2, 3, 4. Revised Edition, pp. 2, 3.
[45]Lacey, *op. cit.*, p. 16. Revised Edition, p. 14.

of polyandry, is thus seen to be contrary to natural law."[46] Polygamy is either simultaneous or successive.[47]

Therefore, remarriage after divorce, once, or even twice, is successive polygamy. This is becoming more and more of a convention which is acceptable to our society, viz., that one may have two or even three spouses provided one has them successively or one at a time.

Canon Lacey states that simultaneous polygamy "has never obtained a recognized standing in Christendom."[48] His position directly contradicts the position of Dr. Jones, *supra*:

> In the absence of any express prohibition of polygamy, it is invariably assumed by the writers of the canonical books of the New Testament, and by the constant witness of the Christian Church, that monogamy is the rule. It is assumed in the condemnation of marriage after divorce; for, if it were lawful to take a second wife while retaining the first, it would *a fortiori* be lawful to take a second after repudiating the first. It may be taken for certain that the lack of any express prohibition is due to the fact that the practice of polygamy was unknown among those to whom the Gospel was preached.[49]

Of successive polygamy or remarriage after divorce, Canon Lacey declares that, though "less odious" than simultaneous polygamy, a law which recognizes it must be condemned:

> It is not so much an infraction of the divine law as an impotent pretence, an attempt to alter a fact of nature, and a denial of the existence of that which exists. It may be compared with a law which should purport to destroy the kinship of a brother and sister, of a parent and a child.[50]

---

[46] *Op. cit.*, pp. 15, 16. Revised Edition, p. 13, 14.
[47] *Op. cit.*, p. 102. Revised Edition, p. 88.
[48] *Op. cit.*, p. 102. Revised Edition, p. 88.
[49] *Op. cit.*, p. 13. Revised Edition, p. 11.
[50] *Op. cit.*, p. 103. Revised Edition, p. 89.

Canon Lacey's position is not one which rests upon the idea that our Lord was legislating, as Bishop Gore believed, but upon natural law and the light of Revelation which our Lord Jesus Christ gives to it. This is the Anglican philosophical basis for the principle of indissolubility in the Book of Common Prayer.[51]

> A revelation from God will not, therefore, proclaim a new law; the will of God has been imposed on nature from the first, and the divine law was legible in nature, however imperfectly read. We must not suppose a less perfect law of nature superseded or completed by a more perfect law of revelation. The divine law is one and continuous, in nature and in revelation. *The divine law of marriage is nothing else but the order of nature. Revelation does but enable us to understand it more perfectly.** (*Op. cit.*, p. 6. Revised Edition, p. 5.)

Again, on p. 18, he says:

> Because it is constituted in the order of nature, and not only at the will of the parties, it is indissoluble except by an event equally in the order of nature; and this can be found only in death. By virtue of nothing short of this can the husband cease to be husband, or the wife cease to be wife. (Revised edition, p. 15.)

Canon Lacey points out that St. Paul rules peremptorily on marriage and divorce, according to I Cor. 7:10-11. In Romans 7:1-3 the Apostle recognizes that there existed a Christian law, based undoubtedly upon a saying of Jesus. Referring to the accounts in the 10th Chapter of St. Mark and the 19th Chapter of St. Matthew and our Lord's reply to the question about divorce, Canon Lacey continues:

> He answered by a reference to the primary institution

---
[51] See *infra*, p. 106 "Lambeth on Marriage".
*Italics mine.

of marriage, by which man and woman become 'one flesh', deducing the consequence, 'what God joined together let not man put asunder'. . . .

It is to be observed that this teaching of our Lord is expressly based on the natural institution of marriage. He is not giving a new law to Christians. He is enforcing and explaining the natural law which had been corrupted through man's hardheartedness. On this ground divorce is explicitly forbidden; and further, if divorce takes place *de facto*, marriage of the divorced is forbidden as involving the guilt of adultery. That is to say, in spite of divorce the natural relation, the *vinculum*, remains intact. If it were not so, union with a divorced woman, however strongly condemned on other grounds, could not be called adultery.[52]

Canon Lacey believes in the textual authenticity of the Matthean Exception but thinks "it is not improbably a gloss, inserted by the evangelist, calling attention to a practice recognized in the Church when he wrote." The Canon believes, however, that "the excepted cause justifies only the separation of husband and wife . . . and does not affect the subsequent judgment that the marriage of the divorced is adulterous. . . . So it was understood without hesitation by all Christian writers commenting on the words, until the entanglement of the Church with the Empire in the fourth century moved men to find some common ground for Christian teaching and Roman law."[53]

In accord: Watkins, *op. cit.*, pp. 177, 226; also Dr. Gwynne, see *Divorce in America*, p. 84 and *Holy Matrimony and Common-Sense*, p. 151.

(3) The Rev. Felix L. Cirlot, Th.D., Rector of All Saints' Church, Indianapolis, Indiana.

His views are fully expressed in his very fine book, entitled *Christ and Divorce* (1945, Trafton Publishing Co., Lexington,

---

[52] *Op. cit.*, pp. 22, 23, 24. Cf., the Revised Edition, pp. 21, 22.
[53] *Op. cit.*, p. 24.

Ky.), in which he deals with the ideas of Dr. Easton, Dr. Grant, and Dr. Jones. His arguments are technical, involved, and in great detail. No one, however, should consider himself abreast with modern scholarship in our American Episcopal Church on this difficult problem of marriage and divorce, until he has studied this book. A brief introduction to some of the main ideas of this book should be of value.

In Chapter I, the author deals with the problem of the correct text of our chief sources on the question of what our Lord said on this subject. Dr. Cirlot comes to the conclusion that the Matthean Exception refers only to the fact that a man who divorces his wife causes her to commit adultery, either through remarriage or harlotry, for in the days of our Lord there was no other way for her to live. He states that, so far as the exceptive clause is concerned, there is no question raised really as to the right of the husband to remarry. Certainly, this is the sense of Mt. 5:32. He does not make his wife an adulteress, if she is already one.

Dr. Cirlot points out that about 75 percent or 80 percent of the manuscripts on Mt. 19:9 read differently from Mt. 5:32 and add the words "and shall marry another" after the Matthean Exception; they also add "committeth adultery" (Mt. 19:9), i.e. for remarrying unless he divorced his wife for adultery. However, about 20 percent or 25 percent of the manuscripts,[54] including the famous Vatican Manuscript B. render Mt. 19:9 like Mt. 5:32. This author agrees with Dr. Easton that "if we read 19:9 with the bulk of the manuscripts, we get the un-Jewish assertion that the man who remarries commits adultery."[55] So Dr. Cirlot believes that the minority of manuscripts on Mt. 19:9 give the correct text. Therefore, according to this view, there is nothing either in Mt. 5:32 or Mt. 19:9 which authorizes the remarriage of the offended

---
[54]Cf.. the American Revised Version of the Bible.
[55]*Op. cit.*, p. 6.

husband. The author of St. Matthew's Gospel has merely recast what he found in Q into a more truly Jewish form. Dr. Cirlot would have us know that here is

> ... a more completely adequate explanation of why the 'exception-clause' was for several centuries unanimously interpreted as assigning the only cause for which separation from one's wife was allowable, and never by anyone as naming a ground on which remarriage after such separation was permissible.[56]

Dr. Cirlot sees no reason to doubt the authenticity of the second clause of the logion (Mt. 19:9), i.e., "And whoso marrieth her which is put away doth commit adultery."

". . . the account in Matthew," Dr. Cirlot believes, "is historically superior to that in Mark," because he thinks that Matthew relied primarily on Q or on M for his information, though he recast it into Jewish form. It also shows, according to his opinion, that Mark also used Q.[57]

He says:
> ... the Q version would be at every point the form of the narrative which seems to possess superior claims to historicity.[58]

In reply to Dr. Easton's attack on this saying of Jesus as being unhistorical in all its forms, Dr. Cirlot points out that though he agrees with Dr. Easton as to the unhistorical nature of the Matthean form of the first clause of the logion (because Matthew recast Q), he can not agree with him in holding that "the logion is unhistorical even in the form in which it appears in Lk. 16:18, and which we decided above to be substantially identical with the form in which it occurred in the Q source of Mark 10:12 and Mt. 19:9."[59]

---
[56] *Op. cit.*, p. 11.
[57] *Id.*, p. 17.
[58] *Id.*, p. 17.
[59] *Id.*, p. 26.

Dr. Cirlot makes the highly significant statement that Matthew, though failing "to grasp fully the complete equality of woman with man as implied by our Lord's language," has not changed, "but has carefully preserved, even in his revised form of the logion, the truth of the indissolubility of marriage, which is the point with which our Lord was primarily concerned in this logion."[60]

Dr. Cirlot shows that it is absurd to attack this saying of Jesus as not genuine, on the ground that Jesus, as a Jew, could have used the word "adultery" only in the narrow meaning of Lev. 20:10. The attitude of Jesus "would be that it is sheer nonsense—and worse—to say that for a wife to cohabit with a man other than her husband is adultery, but for a man to cohabit with a woman other than his wife is not adultery." (*Id.* p. 28.)

Then Dr. Cirlot says:

> Whether we take the Q account as I have been reconstructing it, or the Markan account, or the isolated verse which is all St. Luke gives us on the subject, or the short 'Matthean' version in the Sermon on the Mount or the longer 'Matthean' version ... we get the same teaching of the indissolubility of marriage, without any exception whatsoever, which we find to have been also the teaching of the New Testament Church as exhibited in St. Paul, who explicitly says he is basing his ruling on the teaching of Christ, and who is decisively confirmed by the fact that for at least three centuries, if not longer, not a single orthodox Church writer, let alone one of repute, can be found to favor or even to tolerate the view that it is possible for the spouse of a living partner, though divorced by human law, to remarry without committing adultery.[61]

Having discussed the problem of the correct text and what the historical Jesus said on this subject, Dr. Cirlot then deals with

---
[60] *Id.*, p. 37.
[61] *Op. cit.*, pp. 22-23; cf. *idem*, p. 142-3.

the meaning of the saying, giving cogent reasons for believing that our Lord taught "not simply that marriage never should be dissolved, and that it is a great sin to dissolve it, but that it is indissoluble, and therefore an impossibility to dissolve it."[62]

Although Dr. Cirlot does not refer to Canon Lacey's book, he is in accord with him in holding that our Lord was not legislating on this subject and, therefore, was not promulgating a positive law but only making clear the law of nature.[63] Dr. Cirlot wisely says:

> . . . we cannot allow remarriage in any case, however exceptional, without surrendering the whole principle of indissolubility.[64]

Of course, he accepts the true doctrine of nullity, and, in his words above, is referring to cases where a valid bond of marriage has been formed. Dr. Cirlot truly declares that:

> . . . the tendency of the doctrine of the dissolubility of marriage is to increase greatly the number of divorces and broken homes. On the other hand, the tendency of the doctrine of indissolubility is to hold such cases down to an absolute minimum.[65]

Dr. Cirlot also deals with the present popular view that our Lord's words on this subject are not to be taken at their face value. This viewpoint has been expressed in several ways but in whatever form objections to the doctrine of indissolubility take, they all have this in common: ". . . they all agree in denying that our Lord's divorce teaching is to be taken as 'law' or 'legislation.' "[66]

---

[62]*Op. cit.*, p. 42. Cf. Canon Lacey, *supra*.
[63]*Id.*, p. 160.
[64]*Id.*, p. 164.
[65]*Id.*, p. 166.
[66]*Id.*, p. 69.

Dr. Cirlot shows that how we are to interpret a saying of our Lord depends on the underlying principle involved. In regard to this logion, the underlying principle is the indissolubility of marriage, as a law of nature, which Dr. Cirlot considers "a theological truth; or, in other words, a true proposition in Christian ethics and moral theology."[67] In connection with the idea that our Lord was merely holding up an ideal for those in matrimony, Dr. Cirlot declares that to refrain from committing the grave sin of adultery, which our Lord said remarriage after divorce constitutes, appears hardly an ideal but rather as the absolute moral minimum.

In answer to Dr. Stowe, Dr. Cirlot admits that there are at present two divergent positions formally held and taught and practiced within the Catholic Church. But he maintains that the facts of history do not justify claiming for the modern Eastern position the title of "*a* Catholic position" nor withholding from the Western and original position the vital title of "*the* Catholic position." He says, "There can be no doubt that before the *new* view developed in the East, the doctrine of the indissolubility of marriage was *the Catholic view*." And the coming into existence of the *later* divergence cannot make it otherwise to-day.[68]

(4) The Rt. Rev. H. St. George Tucker, D.D., Retired Presiding Bishop.

In an editorial in *The Southern Churchman* (July 17, 1937), Bishop Tucker, after referring to the very liberal proposal of the Joint Commission on Marriage and Divorce to allow a bishop at his discretion to grant permission for the remarriage of divorced persons, says:

> This proposal seems to me to be contrary to what has been always regarded as our Lord's teaching. . . . The

---
[67] *Id.*, p. 69.
[68] *Id.*, p. 151.

assumption underlying all the New Testament references to marriage is that its indissolubility is a divine law. One can further assume that this divine law is not simply arbitrarily imposed on mankind but that it represents what will best promote the moral and spiritual welfare of human society. *Any proposal, therefore, which does away with the principle of the indissolubility of marriage not only contradicts what the Church has always acknowledged as a divine law but also substitutes for it human opinion as to what would best promote moral and spiritual welfare....** There has been great dissatisfaction with the present canon. ... However, the new proposal is much more than an attempt to do away with these grounds of dissatisfaction. It would seem to destroy the very principle upon which the present canon is based. I hope, therefore, that if it is presented to the General Convention for consideration that it will be overwhelmingly defeated.

There is no reason to believe that Bishop Tucker has changed his convictions about the indissolubility of marriage since 1937.

(5) The Sanctity of Marriage Association.

This Association stood resolutely for the absolute indissolubility of marriage and fought a valiant fight to eliminate the Matthean Exception from the old marriage canon. Its published ideals called for "complete loyalty to the teaching of our Lord, as witnessed by Holy Scripture and the universal voice of the Primitive Church testifying to the indissoluble character of the marriage bond, 'till death' ". These ideals made allowances for legal separation, and for annulment on the basis of causes preceding marriage "as in the case of sexual impotence, imbecility, fraud, etc." Members of this Association also pledged themselves to work for the elimination of the Matthean Exception in our old Canon, which provided for the remarriage of the innocent party in a divorce for adultery.

The following names appear on the old bulletins of this As-

---

*Italics mine.

sociation, making it possible to list them as members of the School of Indissolubility:

1930—President of the Association, The Very Rev. Milo M. Gates, D.D., Dean of the Cathedral of St. John, New York; Members of the Executive Committee: The Rt. Rev. W. T. Manning, D.D., Bishop of New York; the Rt. Rev. E. A. Stires, D.D., Bishop of Long Island; Dean H. Fosbroke; the Rev. F. W. Tompkins, D.D.; on the Editorial Committee: The Rt. Rev. P. M. Rhinelander, D.D.

1928—Executive Committee: The Rt. Rev. W. A. Guerry, D.D., Bishop of South Carolina; the Rt. Rev. Paul Matthews, D.D., Bishop of New Jersey; on the Editorial Committee: the Rt. Rev. Irving P. Johnson, D.D., Bishop of Colorado; the Rt. Rev. A. C. A. Hall, D.D., Bishop of Vermont.

1920—Executive Committee: the Rt. Rev. F. Burgess, D.D., Bishop of Long Island.

During these years the moving spirit of this Association was its devoted general secretary and treasurer, the late Rev. Walker Gwynne, D.D., of Summit, New Jersey.

The passing of this Association, which was probably due to the death of Dr. Gwynne, signified undoubtedly the end of organized support in the American Episcopal Church for the absolute indissolubility of marriage. Thus the way became smooth for the efforts which were being made looking toward the liberalization of the canon so as to permit the remarriage of divorced persons.

(6) Other Scholars.

The Rt. Rev. Kenneth E. Kirk, D.D., Bishop of Oxford, author of *Marriage and Divorce* (Hodder and Stoughton 1948); the Rev. G. H. Joyce, S.J., *Christian Marriage* (Sheed and Ward 1948); the Rev. O. D. Watkins, *Holy Matrimony* (Rivington, Percival & Co., 1895).

These three scholars stand firmly for the historic principle of the indissolubility of marriage and their books should be carefully studied by those who wish to pursue the subject exhaustively. Fr. Joyce, a reliable Roman Catholic scholar, describes his book as "An Historical and Doctrinal Study", and acknowledges his indebtedness to Watkins' *Holy Matrimony*. The latter is recognized by many scholars as an outstanding Anglican authority and is often quoted by them.

Suffice it to say that one should not come to any final conclusions concerning the mind of Christ on marriage and divorce without at least a passing knowledge of these scholarly works.

Bishop Kirk has said:

> There is, as we have seen, no New Testament basis whatever for the suggestion that our Lord sanctioned remarriage during the lifetime of the first partner even in the case of an 'innocent' person who has secured a divorce . . . our review of the synoptic evidence shows that there is an extraordinarily strong New Testament tradition that He emphatically condemned remarriage after divorce in all cases. This tradition appears not only in the Synoptists, but also in S. Paul. . . . S. Paul introduces his startling innovation without the slightest apparent recognition of its revolutionary character. He quotes it as a word of the Lord which will be accepted as such without challenge. Both these facts go far to prove that long before the synoptic tradition had been reduced to its present form, and within twenty-five years of the Crucifixion itself, there was absolute unanimity in the Church that our Lord had proclaimed the indissolubility of marriage. . . . There are those who profess to find it almost incredible that our Lord should have spoken so explicitly on the subject of marriage. The answer to this is simple: the attitude of the early Church in the matter makes it even more incredible that He should *not* have done so.[69]

In connection with the dangers involved in nullity cases, Bishop Kirk declares:

---
[69]*Marriage and Divorce.* pp. 70, **71**, 72.

But nullity is a sphere into which none but the expert can venture; and many alleged 'hard cases' prove undeserving of sympathy when the evidence is sifted by the trained eye. To allow amateurs to dabble in these matters would almost certainly result in decisions so contradictory and ill-advised that grave dissatisfaction and even scandal would ensue. (*Idem p.* 131.)

He also discusses the question as to whether or not our Lord was legislating or stating an ideal. He points out the pitfalls involved in the latter viewpoint.[70]

In view of the following quotation from *The Reason of Life* by William Porcher DuBose, M.A., S.T.D., University of the South, Sewanee, Tennessee, there is no doubt about the fact that this great theologian also belongs to the School of Indissolubility:

> Human life is possible only in society: the individual lives only in the common life and *is* only as he enters into and fulfills its natural relations, shares its aims, ideas. . . . Unity and community is the essence and condition of life: and it originates in the union and communion of man and woman in the closest of bonds, grows into the unity of the family, and widens from that into the oneness of the clan, the state, the nation, and humanity. . . . The Christian law and ideal of marriage is as much part, and highest part, of nature's institution of the sex relation, as reason and freedom were part of nature's original institution of man. . . . Who will claim that when youthful pleasure ceases, and domestic utilities have come to an end, nothing more remains of the marriage relation? . . . Is the helpmate to be a mate only in the lowest and not also in the highest functions of life, co-heir of the grace of eternal life as well as sharer of the pains and toils and experiences upon the way to it? All a man's personal, moral, and spiritual selfhood comes out in relation and association and correspondence with other selves, in mutual knowledge and love . . . and the

---

[70] See *idem* p. 72 ff.

true intercourse and mutual complementing of the sexes, for which the difference was instituted, is the root and source and fountain of all that is most beautiful and elevating and noble, as well as of all that is most natural and elemental, in human life. When the marriage relation shall have been degraded into a consent for temporary pleasure and convenience, human life, in all that is worth propagating, will have withered up from the root.[71]

4. An Evaluation.

A careful study of the two Schools of thought, *supra*, will enable one to come to the conclusion that the argument from natural law and Revelation, as given by our Lord Jesus Christ, for the absolute indissolubility of marriage is overwhelming and points to the pressing need of a reaffirmation of our loyalty to the mind of Christ on this difficult problem of the remarriage of divorced persons. The underlying principle of Canon 18, Section 2(b), is the underlying principle of the Marriage Service in the Prayer Book, i.e., the indissolubility of marriage as a status, a relationship or a fact, in the order of nature, which it is impossible to undo. Therefore, it would seem that Bishop Conkling is in error when he says that the principle of this Canon is extended nullity, which is but another name for absolute divorce.[72] Also Bishop Davis is in error when he says that "the pastoral approach ... to the question of marital failure" is the underlying principle.[73]

When our Lord goes back to the original purpose of God and speaks of marriage as a physical relationship in the order of nature, "they twain shall be one flesh", he would not have us, I am sure, think of marriage only as a physical relationship. It is true that the joining of man and woman in matrimony is like the hub of a wagon wheel—the physical and indispensable means

---

[71] Pp. 107 and 108.
[72] *Supra*, p. 48.
[73] See *Journal of the General Convention* 1949, p. 437.

that it could have originated only as an important part of the teaching of our Lord Himself.

Our purpose in setting forth the above classification, i.e., the School of Divorce and the School of Indissolubility, aside from the value of examining modern or 20th century viewpoints on the subject, is to dispel the notion which has spread throughout our Church that the traditional doctrine of the absolute indissolubility of the bond of marriage is outmoded and that the only viewpoint acceptable to modern scholarship is that of Dr. Easton *et al*. We will demonstrate that the convictions of members of the School of Indissolubility are in full accord with the Catholic Church of the early centuries. The Church of England, in spite of minor deviations from this position during the Middle Ages, has been on the whole loyal to this position of the Primitive Church. This is the Catholic position, which is in our Prayer Book, and to which we should adhere. The Catholic view, therefore, which should dominate our thinking on this problem, is the view of the Primitive Church. It is a grievous mistake to be greatly influenced by Rome and Eastern Orthodoxy on this issue as have members of the Joint Commission on Holy Matrimony of the General Convention.

It is proper to point out that the words of Bishop Davis, *supra,* on marriage and divorce indicate the presence of a serious inconsistency in his thinking. We remember that Arius, though undoubtedly a sincere man, freely admitted the deity of Christ; yet he turned right around, so to speak, and denied it, saying that Christ is of a lesser substance than the Father, a sort of demi-god. This in effect was a denial of the full divinity of our Lord. In a similar manner Bishop Davis has spoken of the indissolubility of marriage: "A God-made marriage is and should be indissoluble. That is Christ's teaching. Such a marriage can not be terminated."[78] Yet, he says in effect that only

---

[78]*Supra.* p. 46.

happy marriages are indissoluble and assumes that unhappy marriages are all or nearly all the kind of marriages which never were true marriages anyway. "But most marital failures were never true marriages in the Christian sense. The couples were not free and competent to make a Christian marriage or there were physical and mental impediments that became apparent later."[77] We also remember that he said in the Report of the Special Committee, *supra*: "Two points of view are legitimate: one, that if one or more of the impediments existed before marriage, no marital bond was created; the other, that if one of the impediments arises after marriage, the marital bond is broken."[78] It is a very serious matter that the House of Bishops failed to condemn this Report of the Special Committee in 1949.

Anyone who states that two points of view on the person of Christ are permissible in this Church, i.e., the doctrine of Arius and the doctrine of Athanasius,[79] in effect does not really believe in the deity of our blessed Lord Jesus Christ. With full admission of the sincerity of Bishop Davis, it is, nevertheless, obvious that he does not believe in the indissolubility of the marriage bond in the historic sense of the term.

Likewise, it is difficult to reconcile the statements made by Bishop Conkling. For example, it was at his suggestion that the House of Bishops (1949) adopted this resolution: "Resolved, That the House of Bishops reaffirm the statement adopted by the last General Convention[80] 'that *the Church's steadfast purpose is to hold to its traditional position** on Christian marriage and that present changes are to strengthen this purpose and more perfectly to attain the Christian ideal.' " (Journal of the General Convention 1949, p. 72.) Yet he favors

---
[77]*Supra*, p. 46.
[78]*Supra*, p. 46.
[79]The Nicene Creed expresses the convictions of Athanasius.
[80]Adopted only by the House of Bishops in 1949.
*Italics mine.

the doctrine of extended nullity, which was unknown in the Early Church and also in the Church of England after the Reformation.

The words and doctrines of these two Bishops have had much to do with the creation of the present state of confusion which exists in the Church today.

The main position, however, of the School of Divorce remains to be considered, aside from the technical questions of texts and sources. It is one which can not lightly be dismissed, namely, that our Lord was not legislating but setting up an ideal. All of us feel the appeal and the pressure of this position, especially as we remember the times when we have been face to face, in pastoral interviews, with unhappy and unfortunate persons whose marriages have ended in the divorce courts.

It has been shown, however, hereinabove, beyond any reasonable doubt, that our Lord definitely was not legislating or merely holding up an ideal but was revealing the original purpose of God by referring to the Divine Will or Divine Law in Gen. 2:24, which means that when two persons, male and female, have been made "one flesh", it is a fact; the basis and means of bringing about all of the most wonderful relationships of life, i.e., those of the family. "What therefore God has joined together" in this relationship of the bond of holy marriage can not be dissolved except by death.

Consequently, Canon Lacey is on solid ground, indeed, when he insists that marriage is a fact in the order of nature. When this bond of matrimony is once truly formed, no man nor court is really capable of undoing the fact that the woman is the mother of her husband's children, and he the father of her children. Their relationship, while it can be dreadfully impaired, can no more be dissolved, except by death, than can the relationships of father and son, brother and sister. Not even our Lord can dispense a person from the obligations arising from such a bond, because he could not approve that which is inherently wrong. If he could, why then did he allow no loophole or dispensation? The only way in which we could possibly justify the idea that he did provide for such a dispensation is to declare, as does the School of Divorce, that his words are not to be taken at their face value because he was not referring to a divine law; he was only holding up the ideal of a happy lifelong marriage.

Of course, a relationship or bond of matrimony can be so seriously impaired by selfishness, cruelty, and other sins, that separation is the only solution. However, a careful study of the words of our Lord and of the situation in which he uttered them, and also of the words of St. Paul, will demonstrate that the historic position of the Church on the indissolubility of marriage has been the correct interpretation. Our Lord, after recognizing this principle of indissolubility, merely added the inevitable conclusion, i.e., that remarriage after divorce is adultery.

Dr. Easton looks upon this conclusion, which is found in Mark 10:11-12, Luke 16:18, and Matthew 5:32, as not being an authentic statement which was made by our Lord. He thinks that these references constitute "very early interpretations of the Church" about what our Lord had said on marriage according to Mark 10:2-9.[81]

It is possible to admit, for the sake of argument, that this position is sound. Even if it is, however, the principle of the indissolubility of marriage still stands, for it primarily depends upon what our Lord said according to Mark 10:2-9 and not upon the conclusion in Mark 10:11-12 that remarriage after divorce is adultery. It is very difficult, in view of the language of this passage (i.e. Mk. 10:2-9), to interpret it other than as an unveiling by our Lord of God's natural law. We are convinced,

---

[81]See *supra*, pp. 38-39.

however, that this conclusion is our Lord's own authentic interpretation. St. Paul's clear-cut statements in Ro. 7:1-3, I Cor. 7:10-11, and Ephesians 5:31-32, are impressive support for such a position.

Apart from Revelation, there is ample evidence of a natural law of God governing marital relations. For example, Westermarck, author of the monumental work, *The History of Human Marriage,* and one time professor of sociology at the University of London, made extensive researches into the marital customs and sociological problems of the human race all over the world.

This great sociologist points out that there is in nature a fundamental relationhip between durability of marriage and the protection and care of the young upon which depends the very existence of the species. This protection is provided for in nature through the providence of God, because it is the duty and primary obligation of the mother to nurture her children. A study of nature reveals the fact that where the offspring are few in number and also require a considerable time to mature, the parents tend to remain together long after the sexual act of propagation in order to fulfill this duty. On the other hand, there is nothing which even appears to be marriage among such species as fishes, snakes, and the lower insects. The reason is obvious: the offspring can swim, fly, or wiggle around immediately after birth and provide for themselves. Among birds, therefore, which lay a small number of eggs, there is at least a temporary type of marriage for the protection and care of the mother and her offspring. Among some species of birds there appears to be a lifelong type of marriage.

Those who have studied the habits of gorillas testify, according to Westermarck, that there was "almost always one male and one female", and with the pair a young one. An old male gorilla has been known to warn his family of the approach of an enemy with a wild yell, lead them out of danger, and return to make an attack. Gorillas live in some kind of family groups, the very natural and obvious reason being that the female produces only one offspring at a time, and one which requires some time for development.

Westermarck says that a study of the habits of marriage among mankind reveals the universal occurrence of the same phenomenon:

> Among the lowest savages, as well as the most civilized races of men, we find the family consisting of parents and children and the father as the protector and supporter ... the hypothesis of a primitive stage of promiscuity not only lacks all foundations in fact, but is utterly opposed to the most probable inference we are able to make as regards the early conditions of man. ... From what has been said it appears that marriage and the family are most intimately connected with one another: it is originally for the benefit of the young that male and female continue to live together. We may, therefore, say that *marriage is rooted in the family rather than the family in marriage.**
> Sensual love is fickle; it is distinguished by a desire for change. On the other hand, when love implies sympathy and affection arising from mental qualities, there is a tie between husband and wife which lasts long after youth and beauty are gone. This leads to monogamy that is enduring. *Monogamy is the only form of marriage that is permitted among every people.** Whenever we find polygamy, polyandry or group-marriage, we find monogamy side by side with it.[82]

As we have seen from Canon Lacey's statement above, polygamy and polyandry are both against nature and, therefore, against the well-being of the race. Even among races which permit polygamy the custom is not widespread for this reason and

---
*Italics mine.
[82] *Op. cit.*, Vol. I, pp. 37, 38, 72, 104.

also because of the economic requirements of polygamy; only a few wealthy men of any race can afford to support several wives and their children. Polyandry, a woman married to several men, and group-marriages (a group of men and women married together promiscuously) are even more against nature than polygamy, for no one in the community knows whose children the offspring are; these, therefore, are much rarer forms of marriage than polygamy.

The fixing of responsibility for the nurture of children and for the protection of their mother is fundamental in the life of all races, and even true among savages. Therefore, everywhere in the world there are to be found regulations governing the marital relations of men and women. Thus Dr. Easton, *supra*, p. 37, is apparently in error when he implies that the problem of marriage and divorce was among the Jews and Romans merely a personal affair, for even in the absence of any social legislation on the subject, marital customs among every race, in the form of written or unwritten law, have controlled what individuals were permitted to do.

The conclusion which one is bound to draw from Westermarck's discovery of the universality of monogamy is that we have here most impressive evidence of God's original and natural law; i.e., that the nature of a man and the elemental needs of the mother and children require a lifelong relationship. Thus, the principle of the absolute indissolubility of marriage is rooted and grounded, not in the convenience or even romantic happiness of the individual partners to a marriage, but in the primordial needs of the family. Any race of people, therefore, which disregards this fundamental law of nature will soon find themselves with a lower standard of marital customs than those of the most primitive tribes in the world today.

In our own United States, the divorce rate today is higher than even in pagan nations such as Japan. The number of divorces for each 100,000 unit of our population during the past eighty years or more are as follows:[83]

1867	27
1887	47
1906	86
1916	113
1926	154

The Book of the Year for 1950 (Ency. Brit.) gives the following statistics, which shows some decline in the divorce rate since the peak immediately following World War II:

YEAR	ESTIMATES MIDYEAR POPULATION	MARRIAGES NUMBER	RATE	DIVORCES NUMBER	RATE
1870—	39,904,593	352,000	8.8	10,962	0.3
1900—	76,094,134	709,000	9.3	55,751	0.7
1930—	123,076,741	1,126,856	9.2	195,961	1.6
1940—	131,970,224	1,595,879	12.1	264,000	2.0
1946—	141,235,000	2,291,045	16.4	610,000	4.3
1948—	146,113,000	1,802,895	12.3	405,000	2.8

This means that in 1948 there was about one divorce to every four or five marriages.

Additional evidence for the existence of the natural law governing human marriage is to be found in a series of articles entitled, "The Post Reports on Divorce," by David G. Wittels. These appeared in *The Saturday Evening Post* (January and February, 1950), and give the results of a Post-financed survey conducted by Dr. William J. Goode, professor at Wayne University in Detroit. The following quotations reveal the alarming threat in this country to the family as an institution and to our American civilization:

---
[83]See *Divorce. Ency. Brit.*

Here, after more than a year of work, are the results of a Post-financed survey of our biggest national scandal. Based on 425 intimate case histories, it shows what has happened to our *six million** women who have already experienced the tragic upheaval of divorce. . . .

The present number of divorcees means that about one sixth of our adult female population have had their status and lives drastically transformed by the process which, at least legally, changes married women back into single ones again. . . . It must have an even greater effect on future generations, because 40 per cent of them had children at the time of divorce. . . . *The divorce rate in this country has risen 800 per cent in the last few decades until it is the highest in the world** and until nowadays at least one out of five marriages winds up in the divorce courts. That is no longer news; it has widely been viewed with alarm in pulpits, clinics, courtrooms, colleges and the press. . . .

But once upon a time, in practically all those marriages,* there was a romantic period of moonlight and roses. When they said their vows, most of those people took 'until death do us part' sincerely and literally.

The author of these articles lists the main causes for divorce, on the basis of this survey, as follows:

    1. Emotional immaturity, including what has lately been popularized as 'momism'.[84]

    2. Our modern industrial civilization, which has wiped out many of the material reasons for family life.

    3. The idea that romantic love is the main reason and sufficient basis for marriage.

    4. Parental disapproval and mother-in-law trouble.

    5. Differences in background.

    6. Finances and lack of housing.

    7. Jobs for women.

    8. Ambition.

    9. Infidelity.

---

*Italics mine.
*Italics mine.
[84] Derived from Momus, the god of faultfinding in Greek mythology.

It is interesting to note from these articles that sexual incompatibility is not considered a frequent cause of divorce. Undoubtedly, the emotional immaturity which is cited as the primary cause for divorce is not such a defect of personality "as to make competent or free consent impossible";[85] rather it is the result of the lack of parental and personal discipline. Certainly, easier ways to obtain divorces are not a remedy for it. Wittels says " 'emotional immaturity' is so general a term. It is almost like ascribing all crime to the devil in human nature".

The divorcees, who were interviewed for this survey, admitted "that the fault might have been at least partly theirs. Frequently, the real reason for divorce was very different from what appeared in the legal records". Many of these divorcees revealed the fact that most of them had discovered that a divorce proved to be an unsatisfactory and often an unhappy solution to marital troubles; and often wished that they had accepted the thorns of married life along with the roses.

In an obvious reference to natural law Wittels, referring to the idea that marriage is chiefly a matter of romance, says:

> But the idea that it is the main ingredient is comparatively new, largely confined to our Western civilization and most virulently concentrated in this country. The result is that few of our young people realize that there are other purposes in marriage . . . it is necessary[86] to go back to why marriage is the oldest human institution, older even than religion, government and law. Prehistoric men and women teamed up, and not only for mating purposes. . . . A woman needed a protector and provider; a man could do more hunting if he had a partner to take care of the preparation of the food and clothing and other domestic duties . . . it is likely that the 'divorce' rate among those semibrutish ancestors was much lower than it is in this supposedly enlightened era.

---

[85] See Canon 17.
[86] In order to discover why a certain couple broke up he emphasizes the factor of the labor required to produce for the needs of a home in years gone by.

The survey by Dr. Goode, as presented by Wittels, shows the dreadful effect of divorce upon children. It is estimated that we have in our country 5,000,000 children, who have been semi-orphaned by divorce. It has been proved that divorce "scars them for life"; cripples them "emotionally"; and that "it is usually the children who suffer the greatest emotional shock in the breakup of a marriage. The worst blow to them, and the one with the most lasting aftereffects, is the *feeling of rejection*.* . . . 'As a defense against further hurt,' says one expert, 'the rejected child develops a strong resistance against those who have any authority over him'. . . . Criminologists, too, believe that 'the roots of delinquency are to be sought in the emotional rejection of children by one or both of their parents'. . . . Frank J. Hertel, general director of the Family Service Association of America, reports that 53 per cent of delinquent children come from broken homes". (*Id.*)

Wittels, therefore, says: "The effect of divorce upon children is . . . by many times the worst plague which ever struck this country." This author, however, seems to stress too much the division of labor, which marriage in prehistoric times effected and does not emphasize sufficiently the fact that such marriages were primarily grounded in the needs of the family, foremost of which is the protection of the mother for the welfare of the children. From the Christian standpoint, there has been no fundamental change in the primordial needs of the family, although it must be admitted that modern life, with changing economic situations, has placed more stresses and strains upon marital relationships. The Christian nurture of children demands today, more than ever before, stable and permanent marriages.

The great value of Wittels' articles, however, is that they glaringly reveal our national divorce scandal. This whole mess

---

*Italics mine.

indicates that something is basically wrong in our American civilization and in our corporate attitude as Americans toward the problem of marriage and divorce. It all points very clearly to the fact that divorce is not the remedy[87] but, on the contrary, is exceedingly harmful to the fundamental needs of the family. This disgraceful situation is what it is because of disobedience concerning a natural law of God. Of course, these articles have chiefly pragmatical significance, not being at all theological, yet they provide the most up-to-date practical evidence in support of the view that the indissolubility of marriage is a **natural law of God.**

We have also quoted from Westermarck for the same purpose. Probably, he would not have personally objected to some kind of a limited divorce law. Certainly, he recognized the fact that divorce, along with his discovery of the universality of monogamy, has been granted among almost every race, but, of course, never as freely anywhere in the world as in modern America.

The interesting and absorbing point of these references to Westermarck and to Wittels' articles is the impressive evidence from nature, which they furnish (although they do not directly say so) that the indissolubility of marriage is the will of God, which "has been imposed on nature from the first." It is the divine law which was "legible in nature however imperfectly read."[88] It can be perceived by reason alone without the aid of Revelation. Hooker says:

> ... the general principles of the law of reason are of such a character that it is not easy to find men who are ignorant of them. This rational law was formerly commonly

---

[87] One is reminded of the remarks of Lord Bristol in the debate (1669) on the Bill to authorize Lord Roos to remarry after an Ecclesiastical Court had granted him a divorce *a mensa et thoro* on the grounds of his wife's adultery. Lord Bristol on that occasion said. "that he would support a Bill to legitimate issue *post factum* as in the case of the Marquis of Northampton under Edward VI, but not 'a law *a priori* to encourage one to steal his neighbor's mutton, that is to establish wickedness by a law'." See Lacey, *op. cit.*, p. 187. Revised Edition, p. 163.

[88] Lacey, *supra, op. cit.*, p. 57.

called the law of nature, and by it is meant that law which human nature recognizes as that to which it is universally bound by reason. It is also for this reason properly called the law of reason. It includes all those matters which human beings quite obviously know or might know through the light of their natural understanding, to be becoming or unbecoming, virtuous or vicious, good or evil for them to do.[89]

The mind of Christ can best be understood as revealing the eternal and natural law of God. Certainly, He was not merely presenting an ideal or a counsel of perfection for He was dealing with the natural needs of the family. Neither was He legislating or announcing for the first time a positive law.

---
[89]*Hooker's Polity in Modern English* by Dr. John S. Marshall, p. 26.

CHAPTER III

THE HISTORIC POSITION OF THE ANGLICAN COMMUNION ON THE INDISSOLUBILITY OF MARRIAGE

1. THE ANTE-NICENE CHURCH—TO THE TIME OF CONSTANTINE AND THE COUNCIL OF NICAEA 325 A.D.
2. FROM CONSTANTINE TO JUSTINIAN 314-527 A.D.
3. THE MIDDLE AGES—FROM THE TIME OF THE JUSTINIAN CODE (542 A.D.) TO THE REFORMATION
4. FROM THE ENGLISH REFORMATION TO THE PRESENT DAY
5. THE CHURCH OF ENGLAND AND THE PAULINE PRIVILEGE OR PREROGATIVE
6. LAMBETH ON MARRIAGE

THE HISTORIC POSITION OF THE ANGLICAN COMMUNION ON THE INDISSOLUBILITY OF MARRIAGE

WE have dealt at great length and in much detail with 20th Century viewpoints concerning the mind of our Lord on marriage and divorce. This has been deemed necessary in order for us to realize that there is an adequate and completely satisfying philosophical basis, so far as reason, natural law and Revelation can help us, for the historic position of the Anglican Communion concerning this subject. A careful study of the thought of the scholars listed above under the School of Indissolubility should cause many, who have been influenced by the scholars of the School of Divorce and by the modern popular view, to rethink their opinions on this issue. If this book accomplishes this result our efforts will have been justified.

In the light of this philosophical basis and also in view of the historic interpretation of the Anglican Communion through the ages, as expressed in the Marriage Service of the Book of Common Prayer, the principle of the absolute indissolubility of the bond of marriage is fully supported, beyond any reasonable doubt, by the authority of Christ Himself. The historic witness of the Church impressively sustains this view.

It is not the purpose of this Thesis to give a detailed exposition of the history of the Church's position on this principle, based on primary sources, but simply to substantiate our statements concerning the teaching of the Church on the subject from secondary and yet very able and reliable authorities.

The Church of England has been faithful to the essential teaching of the Catholic Church of the first centuries. The Church was firmly established in the British Isles during the time of the Ante-Nicene Church, for British Bishops participated in the Council of Arles in 314 A.D. In order to know the Anglican position, we must be familiar with the position of the Primitive or Early Church. Whatever deviations from ancient doctrine took place in England during the Middle Ages (and here we are surely on solid ground) the Church of England sought during and as a result of the Reformation to return to the purity of life and teaching of the One, Holy, Catholic, and Apostolic Church of the first centuries. Dr. Gwynne says: "It was to that age, when the unwritten tradition of 'the mind of Christ' from the lips of Apostolic and sub-Apostolic men, and the written tradition of at least two of those centuries, was fresh and clear, that our English reformers in the sixteenth and seventh centuries confidently appealed for confirmation of the faith. That also is our only safe rule of interpretation today."[1]

1. THE ANTE-NICENE CHURCH TO THE TIME OF CONSTANTINE AND THE COUNCIL OF NICAEA 325 A.D.

Remarriage after divorce was not permitted in this period. O. D. Watkins, a most reliable authority, has said:

> It is most significant that the testimony of the first three centuries affords no single instance of a writer who approves remarriage after divorce in any case during the lifetime of the separated partner, while there are repeated and most decided assertions of the principle that such marriages are unlawful.
> Reviewing all the cases of remarriage after divorce, we find that the writers and canons of the period which ends with Constantine's conversion do not approve of such remarriage in any case, and that there is considerable expression of disapproval in every case. . . . *If the voice of the earliest Church is to be heard, Christian marriage is altogether indissoluble.**[2]

---

[1] *Holy Matrimony and Common-Sense* p. 152; see also pp. 109. 113.
*Italics mine.
[2] *Op. cit.*, pp. 222 and 225. Also Gwynne's *Divorce in America*, p. 122.

HISTORIC POSITION OF ANGLICAN COMMUNION 89

Mr. A. T. MacMillan of the Church of England in his book presents the teaching of his Church on this subject, and succinctly reviews the historical background of the present day situation. Although we can not agree with his main conclusions, which he sets forth in his last chapter, yet we do recommend this work for study. He quotes Watkins on the teaching of the Early Church with absolute confidence. He also says that "there is no instance during this period of any writer referring to Matt. XIX, 9 as to an authority allowing remarriage after divorce, or as to a difficult passage requiring to be explained away."[3]

Dr. Cirlot is in accord with Watkins and says:

> In regard to the question of divorce . . . the teaching of Christ on the subject is clear and decisive. . . . So is the verdict of the *whole* Catholic Church, *in diffuso,* with virtual if not complete unanimity, for at least the first three centuries, and very possibly for the first five. The only reason an Ecumenical Council did not rule on the point was because no dispute on the subject came before such a Council, and these Councils did not make a habit of ruling on undisputed points.[4]

2. FROM CONSTANTINE TO JUSTINIAN—314-527 A.D.

MacMillan says of this period:

> As regards remarriage after divorce, the West is practically unanimous in declining to admit it. In the East the teaching is uncertain, some writers allowing remarriage usually only to the innocent spouse.[5]

He quotes Watkins, *op. cit.,* p. 344, in support of this statement. According to Watkins, the Eastern Churches were already feeling "the pressure of the secular law and of the conventional

---

[3] *Op. cit.,* p. 88.
[4] *Op. cit.,* p. 151.
[5] *Op. cit.,* p. 88-89.

morality of the Eastern Christians", which demanded that a man put away his wife permanently if she committed adultery. He was not allowed to forgive her.

3. THE MIDDLE AGES—FROM THE TIME OF THE JUSTINIAN CODE (542 A.D.) TO THE REFORMATION.

The Eastern Churches definitely yielded to the code issued by Justinian in 542 A.D. and accepted in practice the view that marriage can be dissolved not only by natural death but also by moral and spiritual death;[6] an idea which has profoundly influenced many of those who have worked during the past twenty years for a liberalization of our marriage canon so as to permit the remarriage of divorced persons by the American Episcopal Church. We ought to bear in mind, however, that the Eastern Churches yielded to secular and political power; "the price of ecclesiastical leadership had to be paid in the coin of political entanglement, which, like a disease, infected the whole life of Eastern Christianity."[7]

MacMillan says:

> It is during the period after Justinian that takes place the great and lasting divergence between the teaching of the East and the West . . . the grounds,[8] either defined by the Church or defined by the State and accepted by the Church, are adultery, such acts as are conducive to adultery . . . apostasy of either spouse . . . taking of monastic vows.[9]

We, however, are interested in the position of the Church of England, which was in general the same as the Church of Rome before the Reformation. After the time of Constantine the

---

[6] "An Introduction to the Study of Canon 41" by Frank Gavin *et al.*, p. 7.
[7] *The Divine Commission* by Bp. Wilson, p. 106.
[8] For divorce in the East.
[9] *Op. cit.*, pp. 89-90.

Church in the West began to gain full control over marital questions and issues. This was also true in England. The ecclesiastical courts dealt with all such questions until Parliament passed the Matrimonial Causes Act in 1857 under which jurisdiction was turned over to a secular court, known as the Divorce Court, which followed the ancient rules[10] of the ecclesiastical courts except in cases where statutory grounds for absolute divorce were provided.

This control was gained first in Italy. Watkins says:

> Summing up the traditions of the Roman Church for the second five centuries of Christianity, it may be said that they consistently maintained the early traditions of the indissolubility of Christian marriage with only one certainly discordant utterance: viz., the judgment of Gregory II in the case of supervening infirmity. The peculiar position of the episcopal courts as authorized tribunals, in a condition of affairs where all secular authority was in a state of flux, had the effect of making the strict tradition of the Roman Church the only admitted law of marriage in the Italian peninsula.[11]

Apparently, it was quite a while before the same ecclesiastical control was extended over the rest of the West, but this domination definitely took place by the 10th and 11th centuries.[12]

The late Bishop Hall of Vermont has said:

> About 1148 Gratian published his 'Discretum' (or Concordance of discordant canons). This became the basis of the *Corpus juris canonici.* Gratian maintains throughout the entire indissolubility of the marriage bond when once

---

[10] "The law of marriage in England is based upon the law of the Church, and although Parliament has in more recent times legislated so as to make lawful marriages which are contrary to the law of the Church, the broad principles of the law are those developed by the Church." (MacMillan, *op. cit.,* p. 102.)

[11] *Op. cit.,* p. 380.

[12] See MacMillan p. 91 and Watkins p. 394, *op. cit.*

that bond has been completed by consummation following marital consent; and this teaching has ever since been that of the whole Western Church.[13]

MacMillan sketches the history of the situation in England as follows:

> In the British Isles before the Norman conquest there was, in varying degrees, considerable laxity. For instance, the laws of Howell the Good, insofar as they represent the practice of the Welsh Church in the tenth century, 'touch the lowest point ever reached by Christan legislation in the matter of marriage'. Similar laxities are found elsewhere among the Celtic Churches. The most important of this time is the teaching of Theodore of Tarsus, the Greek Archbishop of Canterbury from A.D. 668-690. Clearly he was influenced by the Eastern teaching and practice, and in his Penitential he definitely admits remarriage after divorce not only for adultery but on many other grounds. . . . In view of the teaching of Theodore of Tarsus, it is worth noticing that the Council of Hertford (A.D. 673, and so held during his archiepiscopate) condemned remarriage after divorce.
>
> From the time of the Norman Conquest the English Church came into line with the Churches of Italy, and the continent, and the Continental Canon Law. 'It may be said that from the time of the Norman Conquest, there has never been any serious contention in England that the law of the English Church embodied any recognition of divorce *a vinculo*, properly so called, or of remarriage after divorce'.[14]

We ought not to be overly disturbed by variations from the doctrine of indissolubility in the West, especially in England,

---

[13] See Gwynne's *Divorce in America*, p. 128.
[14] See *op. cit.*, pp. 91-92. He quotes Watkins, *op. cit.*, p. 423, 426. Cf., *id.*, pp. 394 ff. See also Gwynne's *Divorce in America*, pp. 129-130.

during the Middle Ages, because the Anglican position involves a protest against the abuses of the Papacy and the errors of Rome during this period, and a wholehearted return to the Church of the first centuries.

Under the guise of nullity, which was stretched considerably, all sorts of technicalities in connection with impediments made it possible for the ecclesiastical courts of the Middle Ages to circumvent the indissolubility of marriage. This was largely true of impediments having to do with affinity. Canon Lacey says:

> A stationary population, compelled to look for partners in marriage within narrow limits of neighborhood, was entangled in a complete network of prohibitions, and a genuine necessity made much relaxation necessary. But dispensation, however justifiable, is the worst enemy of law.[15] The Western canonists, who upheld in the letter the strictest observance alike of the natural law and of human law in regard to marriage, indirectly broke down all the safeguards of law. They never moved a hair's breadth from the doctrine of the indissolubility of marriage. . . . But, the intricacy of the law regarding impediments, the strictness with which it was applied, and the frequent occurrence of legal flaws in dispensations granted and received not always in good faith, made an immense number of marriages precarious. . . . The very multiplicity of impediments brought it about that while a marriage could never be dissolved, it could only too often be annulled. . . . It

---

[15] "A single rift in the divine dam of the moral law, just as truly as a single rift in the Church's faith in the Incarnation, leads on logically to the mighty flood that ignores all law and ends in disaster. There is no logical resting place between the easiest of all methods of getting rid of husband or wife and the fifty others provided by our State Legislatures, some harder to endure and to prove than adultery." (See Gwynne's *Holy Matrimony and Common-Sense*, p. 107.) Also note these words of the late Bishop Hall of Vermont: "Whatever difficult questions of interpretation may be raised as to our Lord's declarations concerning marriage, the stricter understanding of them, upheld by the Church generally, seems to be vindicated by the impossibility, proved by experience, of maintaining any other consistent rule." (See Gwynne's *Divorce in America*, p. 133.)

cannot be denied that the medieval canon law failed miserably[16] as guardian of the holy estate.[17]

The modern Roman Catholic Church still follows in a limited way the medieval practice of extended nullity, although the extreme laxity of the ecclesiastical courts of the Middle Ages has been reformed by the Council of Trent 1563. Under the Roman decree of *Ne Temere* (1908), however, even marriages between Roman Catholics and baptized Christians of other Communions are considered null and void. This constitutes the prohibitive impediment of mixed religion (*mixta religio*). This is not to be confused with the impediment of disparity of religion or worship (*disparitas cultus*). "The impediment of *disparitas cultus*, nullifying the marriage of a Christian with an unbeliever, was derived from St. Paul's teaching, and its diriment effect was not based on any conciliar constitution or decretal, but only on general custom. It was never extended in the West, as in the East, to cover the case of heretics." (Lacey, *op. cit.*, p. 154; Revised Edition, p. 133.) Since the decree of *Ne Temere*, however, it has been so extended in accordance with the Roman position but it is not under Roman Catholic law a diriment impediment as is *disparitas cultus*.

The Code of Canon Law, promulgated by Pope Benedict XV (1917), reduced the number of prohibitive impediments to four and cut down the number of diriment impediments from eighteen to thirteen. The number, however, is still entirely too large to be acceptable to the Anglican Church. Also the Church of England does not accept certain types of these impediments, i.e.: a vow not to marry, mixed religion, disparity of religion, sacred orders, etc. The reason is that the Anglican Communion does not forbid its members to marry persons outside of this Church and neither does it look with favor upon

---

[16]Bp. Mortimer edits this passage considerably. Cf. Joyce, *op. cit.*, pp. 388 ff.
[17]*Op. cit.*, Revised Edition, pp. 137, 138.

the enforced celibacy of clergy. Of course, this Church disapproves of a marriage with an unbeliever, but does not consider it to be null and void.

There is much that is fine about the Roman position on marriage and divorce, for the Roman Church stands for the indissolubility of Christian marriage. The trouble, however, with Roman doctrine on marriage and divorce is *its exclusiveness* in regard to other Christians and its misinterpretation of the Pauline Privilege. As Dr. Pottle says:

> The feature of Roman practice that really gives offence, in this as in other matters, is its jealously exclusive position. Abolish the indiscriminate annulment of marriages under the decree of *Ne Temere* and divorces under the more far-fetched applications of the Pauline Privilege, and it is doubtful whether Roman practice[18] would be much criticized by anybody.

It is obvious, however, that we do not want our American Episcopal Church following the Roman practice of extended nullity even though reformed by the Council of Trent. Rather do we desire that the American Episcopal Church remain loyal to the doctrine and discipline of the Church of England since she purged herself of modern and medieval Roman innovations and abuses.[19]

4. From the English Reformation to the Present Day.

The Protestant Reformers did not look upon marriage as a sacrament. Luther felt that it was a matter for the State to handle without meddling on the part of the Church.[20] "I advise", said Luther, "that ministers interfere not in matrimonial questions . . . because these affairs concern not the Church, but

---

[18]The truth of this will be supported by a study of *Christian Marriage* by Joyce.
[19]Our authority for the position of Rome is Charles C. Marshall's article in "An Introd. to the Study of Canon 41," p. 13.
[20]Cf.. MacMillan, *op. cit.,* p. 94.

are temporal things, pertaining to temporal magistrates. . . . Ministers ought only to advise and counsel consciences, out of God's Word, when need requires".[21] On the other hand, Calvin taught that the marital relationship is very sacred, and that, while it should be dealt with by the State, the State was bound to follow "the law of marriage as revealed in Scripture."[21] It appears that the weakness of modern Protestantism in general on the sanctity of marriage is due to the fact that "all the Reformers seemed to have considered adultery and desertion just grounds for divorce; and some were in favor of extending the grounds".[23]

The influence of these Reformers caused at the time of the Reformation some wavering among certain leaders in the Church of England. *The Reformatio Legum Ecclesiasticarum,* which permitted divorce on a number of grounds, was drawn up at the time but it never had the effect of law.[24] One English authority, Sir Lewis Dibdin, has stated:

> . . . the law of the Church of England as to the indissolubility of marriage and the corresponding practice of the English Courts, remained unchanged throughout the period under notice, that is, from before The Reformation, until after the present canons of 1603-4 came into operation.[25]

Canon 107 of 1604 clearly says that a couple who have received a divorce *a mensa et thoro* "shall live chastely and continently; neither shall they, during each other's life, contract matrimony with any other person".

Also it is to be noted that the principle of indissolubility as set forth in the Marriage Service of the Book of Common

---

[21]Lacey, *op. cit.,* p. 169. Revised Edition, p. 146.
[22]MacMillan, *op. cit.,* p. 94.
[23]Dr. Pottle, *op. cit.*
[24]See MacMillan, *op. cit.,* p. 92; also Watkins, *op. cit.,* p. 426.
[25]See MacMillan, *op. cit.,* p. 93.

Prayer of the Church of England excludes the doctrine of divorce *a vinculo matrimonii*. Mr. Justice Vaisey of the High Court of Justice in England has said:

> That divorce from the *vinculum* or mystical tie is totally inconsistent with the precepts of our Church must be quite plain to anyone who reads intelligently the Marriage Service in the Book of Common Prayer. It is only death which can break that tie—so we teach, and so we believe. . . . Do not let us confuse our minds by talking about 'nullity', which is concerned with cases where there is not, and never has been, a marriage at all. Given a marriage, the married relationship is for life. . . . (Quoted from "A Critique" on the Report of the Special Committee of the House of Bishops on Procedure under Marriage Legislation (1949) by the Rev. R. E. Coonrad *et al.*, p. 5. The quotation is from a foreword by Mr. Justice Vaisey to a lecture in 1948 by Prof. Alivisatos of Athens, entitled "Marriage and Divorce in Accordance with the Canon Law of the Orthodox Church".)

It is to be noted that the Matthean Exception is not included in the law of the Church of England. This is a point which is not generally understood. After the Matrimonial Causes Act of 1857 a divorce *a vinculo matrimonii* could be obtained in the secular Divorce Court on these grounds: "By a husband from his wife on the ground of adultery alone, but a wife could obtain a divorce only if the adultery was aggravated by incest, bigamy, cruelty, or desertion, or if he were proved guilty of rape or unnatural crimes."[26]

Changes were made in this law of the land less than thirty years ago:

> In 1923 the inequalities were removed and the wife gained the right to sue for divorce on the single ground of her husband's adultery. By A. P. Herbert's Bill of 1937

---
[26]Dr. Pottle's Notes; in accord: Watkins, *op. cit.*, p. 429.

desertion, cruelty, and insanity were added to adultery as single grounds for divorce. *Meanwhile the Canons of the Church of England have not been changed, and are in formal conflict with the law of the land.*[27]

MacMillan is in accord, for, after a reference to the fact that some English Churchmen accept the Matthean Exception, he says: "It is clear, however, that the law of the Church of England has not been so altered."[28] We wish to reiterate that though Parliament granted a few absolute divorces on the ground of adultery before 1857 and though the secular Divorce Court since 1857 has granted such absolute divorces on statutory grounds, *the Matthean Exception, as authority for the remarriage of the innocent party, has never been a part of the law of the Church of England,* nor of any other national branch of the Anglican Communion, except the American Episcopal Church.

The Anglican Communion has always and everywhere denied that any marriage can be dissolved for cause arising after marriage, with the single exception that the American Episcopal Church did, from 1868 to 1946, allow adultery as a ground for permitting the remarriage of the innocent partner. (See "A Critique" by Coonrad *et al.*, p. 4. In accord: the Bulletin of the Sanctity of Marriage Association, July 1930, p. 19; cf., Gwynne's *Holy Matrimony and Common-Sense*, pp. 34, 85, 99, 107, 113.)

The Convocations of Canterbury and York adopted resolutions in 1936[29] which approved and verified the position of the Church of England on the indissolubility of marriage and which did

---
*Italics mine.
[27] Dr. Pottle's Notes; cf., Watkins *op. cit.*, p. 429.
[28] *Op. cit..* p. 94; in accord: Gwynne's *Holy Matrimony and Common-Sense*, p. 107.
[29] Coonrad *et al* in their "Critique" say that this action was taken in 1938, citing *Acts of the Convocations Since* 1921 (pp. 90 ff—S.P.C.K. 1948).

not alter the law of the Church of England so as to allow the remarriage of the innocent party in a divorce for adultery.[30]

The Report of the Commission on Christian Doctrine, appointed by the Archbishops of Canterbury and York in 1922, which was published in 1938, reaffirmed this Anglican doctrine:

> Marriage stands in a special position because, both as a rite and as a state of life it is not something peculiarly Christian, but rather is an institution of the natural order, which is taken into and sanctified by the Christian Church. The teaching of the New Testament, which clearly has its basis in the teaching of our Lord Himself, implies that marriage is in its own principle a lifelong and intimate union, and that anything short of this falls short of the purpose of God. Marriage so understood has the character which enables St. Paul to draw an analogy between it and the union between Christ and the Church. The above statement expresses the essential principle of marriage, and may be fairly regarded as its theological basis.[81]

Coonrad et al., in their "Critique", *supra*, state that the law of the Church of England forbidding the remarriage of divorced persons as expressed in Canon 107 of 1604 "is recognized in the canons on Matrimony proposed by the Archbishops' Commission reporting in 1946: *The Canon Law of the Church of England*, (S.P.C.K. 1947, pp. 125-126)." They also state that Mr. Justice Vaisey, *supra*, was "an eminent member of the Archbishops' Commission."

To sum up: at the time of the Reformation, after some hesitation, "*the Church of England took a course of her own*,"*[82] avoiding on the one hand the weakness of the Protestant Re-

---
[30]MacMillan, *op. cit.*, pp. 93-94.
[81]Pp. 200-201.
*Italics mine.
[82]MacMillan, *op. cit.*, p. 129.

formers in their disloyalty to the indissolubility of marriage and on the other the Roman abuse of the doctrine of nullity.

5. THE CHURCH OF ENGLAND AND THE PAULINE PRIVILEGE OR PREROGATIVE.

We should not leave this discussion on the teaching of the Church of England regarding marriage and divorce without a consideration of the Pauline Privilege. It is based on St. Paul's words about the departure of an unbelieving spouse: "But if the unbelieving depart, let him depart. A brother or a sister is not under bondage in such cases: but God hath called us to peace".[33]

The problem is whether or not this is definite authority for allowing a Christian spouse to remarry or whether it only means that he is not required to live with his unbelieving mate.

Sometime during the history of the Church, probably not before the 7th Century,[34] this passage gave rise to what is known as the impediment of disparity of religion or worship (*disparitas cultus*).[35] According to the medieval Roman doctrine of extended nullity such a marriage can be dissolved. The idea or claim is that St. Paul taught that only a Christian marriage, i.e., a marriage between two baptized persons can be considered as indissoluble. The Code of Canon Law (1917) of the Roman Church classifies it as a diriment impediment.

Apparently, however, this impediment is a Roman innovation of the Middle Ages. Watkins says of it:

> From the time of Justinian it is on the whole true to say that the tendency was to restore the primitive condemnation of mixed marriages.[36] *For some centuries it would*

---
[33] I Cor. 7:15.
[34] See Dr. Cirlot's *Christ and Divorce*, p. 125. Cf. Joyce, *op. cit.*, p. 475.
[35] Not to be confused with the impediment of mixed religion. The Lambeth Committee on the Church's Discipline in Marriage (1948) did not make this distinction: "A mixed marriage may be: (1) A marriage between a Christian and a non-Christian; (2) A marriage between members of different Christian Communions." (*The Lambeth Conference*, 1948. p. 103.)
[36] I.e., between Christians and unbelievers.

appear that, notwithstanding peremptory prohibitions, a marriage between a Christian and a non-Christian was not regarded as essentially null and void.* As, however, larger powers of discipline were achieved, this result was at length attained, and still remains, under ordinary circumstances, the ecclesiastical law of Western Christendom. The phrase 'under ordinary circumstances' has to be inserted, because the comparatively recent practice of Papal dispensation has introduced exceptions."[37]

Dr. Cirlot states that "the evidence for the use of this privilege in the first seven centuries is so extremely scanty; and the privilege would have been of such immense practical utility if understood as it was later; and the doctrine of Scriptural inspiration then current was so incompatible with the supposition that St. Paul was mistaken that I find myself driven very strongly toward the conclusion that the early Church must have interpreted St. Paul as allowing only separation, but not remarriage."[38]

This impediment is not recognized by the Canon law of the Church of England today, and such "mixed marriages[39] in England are valid".[40] Certainly, this has been true since the Reformation, even though "the old law of the Church of England on this question seems obscure, probably because the question has seldom, if ever, arisen."[41] MacMillan thinks, therefore, that this impediment was abandoned only by accident.

MacMillan's final conclusion, with which we can not agree, is that this impediment should be restored and also that of mixed religion (i.e., a marriage between an Anglican and a member of any other Christian Communion). The latter should be con-

---

*Italics mine.
[37]*Op. cit.*, pp. 572-3.
[38]*Christ and Divorce*, p. 125.
[39]Between Christians and unbelievers—*disparatas cultus*.
[40]MacMillan, *op. cit.*, pp. 56. 82, 97. 124.
[41]MacMillan, *id.*, p. 56.

sidered as a prohibitive impediment unless the non-Anglican accepts the doctrine of indissolubility. This author goes further and makes the radical suggestion that all marriages outside of the Church performed by civil magistrates without definite lifelong vows should be considered as lacking the qualities of a true Christian marriage.[42]

> The law of England admits divorce with right of remarriage in both parties. . . . It seems, therefore that, at any rate in register office marriages, there can be no presumption that the parties intend a Christian, or indissoluble, marriage: it might be said that in this case the presumption was the other way. . . .
> We do most strongly suggest, therefore, that the Church should insist, as a condition of treating a marriage as a valid Christian marriage, that it be celebrated in Church. . . .
> We suggest, therefore, that the Church establish machinery, in the form of some kind of tribunal, to which such cases could be referred, and which, on satisfactory proof that the parties had in fact intended a union dissoluble in certain contingencies, could give effect thereto and declare that their marriage was not, and never had been a valid Christian marriage.[43]

Other than this, MacMillan is loyal to the traditional doctrine of indissolubility. He thinks, however, that the Church of England can do this without being disloyal to her catholicity.

We believe that she will be disloyal and that she will violate her post-Reformation loyalty to the doctrine and discipline of the Early Church. MacMillan's position on the Pauline Privilege is rooted in an exclusiveness akin to the Roman position, and in the false distinction between Christian and secular marriages.[44] The Pauline Privilege may have been the tradition of the universal Catholic Church of the West, but only after that part

---
[42] I.e., the intention of a lifelong and indissoluble union.
[43] MacMillan, *op. cit.*, pp. 137, 138, 141.
[44] See *supra*, p. 9.

of Christendom was completely dominated by the Papacy. The Pauline Privilege, therefore, is essentially a Roman doctrine; at least as far as Western Christianity is concerned.

We also consider it an unwarranted assumption to say that, due to the existence of divorce laws, people who have married outside of the Church intend only a dissoluble union. We believe that most people intend a lifelong union, even when the vows do not contain words to this effect, because marriage is inherently a permanent institution of the natural order. Divorce is in fact a frustration of a deep-seated yearning for one's lifemate and the dreams and hopes of a lifetime. Wittels seems to have found this lifelong intention in the marriages of the divorcees who were interviewed.[45]

In fact, in all monogamous marriages the presumption is that the intention was a lifelong union. Only clear and definite evidence of a contract of concubinage or for a trial marriage should be permitted to upset this presumption. The vital interests of the children of such a marriage demand that our Bishops be exceedingly reluctant to grant permission for remarriage under Impediment Eight of Canon 17.[46] Dr. Gwynne has this to say about such an impediment:

> Another[47] is a secret agreement of the parties to live together only as long as they are pleased to do so which would be concubinage and not marriage. In this case, however, public policy and justice, in Church and State alike, would hold both parties bound, otherwise they would be taking advantage of their own wrongdoing, which is contrary to justice and reason. . . . If only one of the parties had made this mental resolve, and hidden it from the other, the case might be one of fraud, and might render the marriage voidable. But this would be usually impossi-

---

[45]*Supra*, p. 79, e.g., his reference to the romantic period of "moonlight and roses."
[46]See p. 13, *supra*.
[47]Impediment.

ble to prove. (*Holy Matrimony and Common-Sense*, p. 187.)

Canon Lacey also effectively answers MacMillan on this point:

> If two persons contract marriage, for example, in a society or under a system of law which treats the bond as normally dissoluble, it does not follow that they intend a merely temporary union; it is enough that they purpose marriage, though a general opinion which they themselves share erroneously regards the consent as revocable. God has joined them together by a natural bond, though it be supposed that man can put them asunder. Otherwise there would be no marriage except where the truth of the indissolubility of marriage is known and received; there would have been no genuine marriage among the Jews or the other peoples to whom the Gospel was preached. The fact that from the first converts to the Church were received as truly married effectively disposes of this question. Since marriage is a natural institution, it must be taken that those who marry intend the natural union with all its consequences, known or unknown, unless any of these be expressly excluded.[48]

Canon 17, of course, properly withholds the Sacrament of Matrimony from two unbaptized persons, but that does not rule out a consideration of what constitutes a valid secular marriage.

The question remains: did St. Paul mean that a Christian who is married to an unbeliever is entitled to remarry after the departure of the unbeliever? Dr. Cirlot, who at one time was inclined to accept the Pauline Privilege, thinks now "that the case for it is dangerously weak"[49] and believes that the permission is only for separation.

Lacey is in accord:

> The question remains whether the Christian party,

---
[48] *Op. cit.*, p. 27. Revised Edition, p. 25.
[49] *Op. cit.*, p. 125.

being so divorced, is free to marry. St. Augustine, as above noted, says not. The contrary opinion has generally prevailed, but it rests on the supposition that marriage is not naturally indissoluble, which we are now examining. The Apostle himself gives no ruling, and it is probable therefore that he leaves this special case under the general rule that a wife separated from her husband must remain unmarried.[50]

Gore's *Commentary*, p. 496, is in accord with this view; at least the author of the article remains unconvinced that St. Paul intended to make an exception to the principle of indissolubility.

Dr. Tyson believes that, in view of St. Paul's uncompromising interpretation of our Lord's mind on the indissolubility of marriage in this passage (read I Cor. 7:1 ff., *supra*, p. 30) and his advice that they can remain together, the unbeliever being sanctified by the believer, the Apostle considered the marriage a true marriage, and did not allow any exception. Dr. Tyson says:

> In St. Paul's judgment, these two people[51] are either married or not married. Assuming that he regards them as not married; what in that case does he advise the Christian partner to do? . . . he counsels them, if they can mutually

---

[50]*Op. cit.*, pp. 21, 22; cf., Revised Edition, p. 19. Bishop Mortimer says: "I have rewritten the passages dealing with St. Augustine in which Canon Lacey represented him as holding that marriage was dissoluble by natural law and only indissoluble for Christians. I do not think that he held this view." (Preface to the Second Edition.) The Bishop has revised the above quotation by omitting the third sentence therein and substituting the word "possible" for "probable" (also he omits here the word "therefore") in the fourth sentence; he then continues: "But his emphatic assertion that what he is here saying is on his own authority and does not rest directly on that of the Lord makes the conclusion almost inevitable that he is here making an exception to that general rule which comes from the Lord that a husband and wife are not to separate, or, if they do, are to remain unmarried. Certainly this is the interpretation of the passage which has generally prevailed, and the canon law contains a series of provisions governing the remarriage of converts thus separated from their heathen partners. Yet it must be admitted that such an interpretation is inconsistent and irreconcilable with the principle that marriage is naturally indissoluble. It remains a curious and unexplained exception to the general rule."

[51]Assuming, he says, for the moment that a Christian has married a non-Christian, though the probability is that when they married both were non-Christians.

agree, to continue living together as man and wife. What is this but advising them to live in concubinage or fornication? ... Clearly then St. Paul conceived them to be married or he could not have given such advice. ... It would seem ... that St. Paul ... is permitting a Christian spouse under certain circumstances permanently to separate from the heathen partner. (*Op. cit.*, p. 80-82.)

On p. 80 Dr. Tyson also asserts:

It is difficult, if not impossible, to believe that St. Paul, on his own personal judgment, is permitting *divortium a vinculo*.

6. LAMBETH ON MARRIAGE.

This Thesis would not be complete without a presentation of the statements of the Lambeth Conferences on marriage and divorce, especially in view of the amazing claim which has been made by the Special Committee of the House of Bishops on Procedure under Marriage Legislation that the Lambeth Conference of 1948 gave ". . . its approval to the position of our Canons", and that

... the Conference also supports the theory that causes arising after marriage can destroy the bond, for on page 98 of the reports, after affirming the lifelong character of the obligations of marriage for Christians, the Committee says: 'We are, however, bound to admit a union which is indissoluble by divine intention may be wrecked by sin; and that by the sin of one or both of the parties the personal relationship in marriage can be completely destroyed.'[52]

This Lambeth Committee (1948) did express a considerate attitude toward Canon 18, Section 2 (b), but it did so distinctly on the ground of nullity and not on the ground of causes arising after a first marriage:

---

[52] *Journal of the General Convention* 1949, p. 440; see also *supra*, p. 46.

In the United States after much thought, new canons have been adopted (1946) under which the Bishop is authorized to enquire and decide . . . that 'no marriage bond as the same is recognized by this Church exists.' The grounds on which such a decision can be made are wider, to some extent, than the grounds of nullity hitherto recognized by the Church, but *it is the principle of nullity that is involved.**[53]

This same Committee, in an Appendix on Indissolubility, also said:

> The personal relationship in marriage can, in fact, be so completely destroyed[54] as to be equivalent to the dissolution of the marriage bond by death. (*Idem*, p. 104.)

Yet this same Committee also emphatically declared:

> We are, however, agreed that (whatever the theological interpretations) the 'indissolubility of marriage', as declared by our Lord, imposes upon those who marry a lifelong obligation, and that for Christians this obligation has an absolute character. . . . We cannot condone what our Lord condemns.[55]

It should always be remembered, however, that a statement of a Lambeth Committee cannot be quoted as having the authority of a Lambeth Conference, unless such an opinion is incorporated in the Encyclical Letter or in one of the Resolutions, which have been adopted formally in the assembly of the Conference. It is important, therefore, to present succinctly the official declarations of the Lambeth Conferences.

The Lambeth Conferences have all definitely upheld the indissolubility of the marriage bond. The Matthean Exception

---

*Italics mine.
[53]*Lambeth Conference* 1948, p. 102.
[54]I.e., "by the sin of one or both partners." (*Idem*, p. 104.)
[55]*Idem*, pp. 98, 99.

has been recognized in the sense that the right of a National Church to deal with cases involving this Exception has been granted. It is highly probable that any Lambeth Conference in the future will not recognize the validity of the Matthean Exception in the light of modern scholarship.

It is well to point out that the Lambeth Conferences have not accepted the Matthean Exception in the sense of a ground for divorce, but only because it is attributed to our Lord as a special dispensation from him on behalf of the innocent party. The Lambeth Conference of 1908, on the other hand, disapproved, by a small majority, the blessing of the second marriage of such an innocent party by the Church.

We repeat again: in spite of this unfortunate concession by the Lambeth Conferences, the American Episcopal Church has been the only branch of the Anglican Communion to write the Matthean Exception into a canonical permission for the remarriage of the innocent party after a divorce for adultery.

It is most certainly true that no Lambeth Conference, including the Conference of 1948, has ever approved of the radical views on marriage and divorce which have been expressed by the Special Committee of the House of Bishops of the General Convention in their 1949 Report *supra*.

The statements which follow have been taken from the Encyclical Letters and Resolutions of the Lambeth Conferences 1867—1948:

> 1867—There were no statements on marriage.
> 1878—Encyclical Letter:
> ". . . steps should be taken . . . to maintain the sanctity of marriage, agreeable to the principles set forth in the Word of God, as the Church of Christ hath hitherto received the same." (*The Five Lambeth Conferences* 1867-1908. The MacMillan Company 1920, p. 96. No Resolution.)

1888—Encyclical Letter:
"In vital connection with the promotion of purity is the maintenance of the sanctity of marriage. . . . We have therefore held it our duty to reaffirm emphatically the precept of Christ relating thereto. . . . The sanctity of marriage as a Christian obligation implies the faithful union of one man with one woman until the union is severed by death." (*Id.*, p. 108.)

Resolution 4 (A) and (B): "That, inasmuch as our Lord's words expressly forbid Divorce, except in the case of fornication or adultery, the Christian Church cannot recognize Divorce in any other than the excepted case, or give any sanction to the marriage of any person who has been divorced contrary to this law, during the life of the other party." (*Id.*, p. 119.)

"That under no circumstances ought the guilty party, in the case of a divorce for fornication or adultery, to be regarded, during the life-time of the innocent party, as a fit recipient of the blessing of the Church on marriage."

1897—Encyclical Letter:
"The maintenance of the dignity and sanctity of of marriage lies at the root of social purity, and therefore of the safety and sacredness of the family and the home." (*Id.*, p. 184.)
No Resolution.

1908—Encyclical Letter:
"The purity of family life is the basis of all national stability . . . we have felt it to be our duty to reaffirm the principles on the subject of divorce which were laid down by the Lambeth Conference twenty years ago, and to assert our conviction that *no view less strict than this is admissible* in the Church of Christ."* (*Id.*, p. 309.)

Resoluton 39 reaffirms Resolution 4 of 1888.

Resolution 40: "When an innocent person has, by

---
*Italics mine.

means of a court of law, divorced a spouse for adultery, and desires to enter into another contract of marriage, it is undesirable that such a contract should receive the blessing of the Church. (Carried by 87 votes to 84.)" (*Id.*, p. 327.)

1920—Encyclical Letter:

"The fellowship between man and woman in marriage was the earliest which God gave to the human race. 'From the beginning of the Creation,' as our Lord reminded us, God made them male and female. *What our Lord adds about marriage is not given as new legislation, but as a declaration of God's original purpose.** The man and the wife are no longer twain but one flesh: and those whom God hath joined together, man is not to put asunder. *This revelation about God's purpose gives the keynote to all that the Church has to teach about marriage**. . . . Its indissolubility should secure to the children the continued care and love of both their parents,[56] so long as they live." (*Conference of Bishops of the Anglican Communion* 1920. MacMillan Co., 1920, p. 17.)

Resolution 67:

"The Conference affirms as our Lord's principle and standard of marriage a lifelong and indissoluble union, for better for worse, of one man with one woman, to the exclusion of all others on either side. . . . Nevertheless, the Conference admits the right of a national or regional Church within our Communion to deal with cases which fall within the exception mentioned in the record of our Lord's words in St. Matthew's Gospel, under provisions which such Church may lay down."

---

*Italics mine.
[56]The question has been asked: "Where there are children, will not a decree of nullity work as great or greater harm as a divorce?" The answer is that it may do so. Therefore, for this reason an ecclesiastical decree of nullity should seldom, if ever, be granted where there are children of the marriage unless the evidence overwhelmingly proves the existence of an impediment.

1930—Encyclical Letter:
"The beauty of family life is one of God's most precious gifts, and *its preservation is a paramount responsibility of the Church*.* Its foundation is the lifelong union of husband and wife on which our Lord decisively set His seal. . . . Holy marriage is part of God's plan for mankind. *It follows that any community disregards this at its peril.*"* (*Lambeth Conference* 1930. MacMillan Co., p. 21.)

1948—Encyclical Letter:
"The Church will not marry anyone who has been previously married save where no marriage bond as recognized by the Church still exists. It bids its members to uphold faithfully the lifelong obligation of the marriage vow. . . ." (*Lambeth Conference* 1948, p. 25.)

Note: The Report of the Special Committee (1949)[57] says that the word "still" indicates "that the bond did once exist." It is very unlikely that the Lambeth Conference of 1948 intended to reverse a long line of solemn pronouncements by the use of the one word "still". The much more natural interpretation of its meaning is that it covers the possibility of the death of the divorced partner or of a decree of nullity.

Resolution 92: ". . . this Conference desires again to affirm *that marriage always entails a lifelong union and obligation*;* it is convinced that upon the faithful observance of this divine law depend the stability of home life, the welfare and happiness of children, and the real health of society."

Resolution 94 recognizes the doctrine of nullity but not of absolute divorce:
"The Conference affirms that the marriage of one whose former partner is still living may not be celebrated according to the rites of the Church,

---
*Italics mine.
[57] *Journal of the General Convention* 1949, p. 440.

unless it has been established that there exists no marriage bond recognized by the Church."

(Much of the material for this section has been taken from my article in *The Living Church* entitled, "Lambeth on Marriage", August 28, 1949.)

Thus the Lambeth Conferences have based their declarations concerning the indissolubility of marriage upon the original purpose of God as revealed in the words of our Lord and upon the needs of the family as the basic unit of society.

This is the mind of Christ according to the interpretation of the Lambeth Conferences.

CHAPTER IV

AN HISTORICAL SKETCH OF MARRIAGE LEGISLATION IN THE AMERICAN EPISCOPAL CHURCH

1. From 1808 to 1925
2. From 1925 to 1946

AN HISTORICAL SKETCH OF MARRIAGE LEGISLATION IN THE AMERICAN EPISCOPAL CHURCH

HAVING considered the historic Anglican doctrine of the indissolubility of marriage, we now turn to a review of the historical background in the American Episcopal Church of the Marriage Canons of 1946, so as to bring out in bold relief the sharp contrast between the statements of the Joint Commissions on Holy Matrimony and the historic Anglican position as expressed in the Marriage Service of the Book of Common Prayer. It is this inconsistency and conflict of principles which has brought about the present state of confusion in the American Episcopal Church.

1. From 1808 to 1925.

The General Convention of 1808, with only two bishops, fourteen clerical and thirteen lay deputies in attendance, adopted the following resolution:

> The ministers of this Church . . . shall not unite in matrimony any person who is divorced, unless it be on account of the other party having been guilty of adultery.

"The expediency of adopting the English canon concerning marriages" was first urged upon the House of Deputies by the delegation from Maryland as a memorial from their Convention and referred to the House of Bishops. Instead of adopting the English canon, only the foregoing Resolution was approved by the Convention.[1]

This Resolution, however, did not become a part of our canons until the General Convention of 1868, when the Matthean Exception, allowing the remarriage of the innocent party, was in-

---

[1] *Journal of the General Conventions* 1785—1821, p. 254.

corporated in the canonical law[2] of the American Episcopal Church, an action which constituted a distinct departure from the doctrine and discipline not only of the Church of England but of the entire Anglican Communion. Before 1868, however, the Resolution of 1808 must have had its unfortunate influence. The Matthean Exception remained in our canonical law until 1946, but it was the subject of many debates.

Dr. Walker Gwynne says:

> With the exception of the years 1871 and 1907 the canon on marriage has been the subject of amendment or discussion in every Convention since 1868.[3]

During the years 1868—1925 the aggressive forces in the General Convention were composed of those who sought to conform the American Episcopal Church to the rest of the Anglican Communion by asking for the elimination of the Matthean Exception as a ground for remarriage after divorce. An amendment to this effect was adopted by the House of Bishops in 1901, 1904, and 1910 but in 1901 and 1904 it was defeated by a narrow margin in the House of Deputies. In 1910 the House of Deputies postponed consideration of this matter.

In 1913 the same proposal was referred to a Joint Commission "on all matters relating to Holy Matrimony." The Report of this Commission in 1916 began with the following significant statement before it suggested any canonical changes:

> With a view to the plain setting forth of the discipline of the Church relating to Holy Matrimony, as well as to the consideration of the various questions referred to the Commission, *it was thought best first to agree on certain principles which should regulate any legislation concerning*

---

[2]The exact words were: "But this Canon shall not be held to apply to the innocent party in a divorce for the cause of adultery." *Journal of the General Convention* 1868, p. 139.
[3]*Holy Matrimony and Common-Sense*, p. 109.

*marriage, and the following Statement of Principles, after full discussion, was approved by the Commission.**

In this Statement the Commission reaffirmed the indissolubility of marriage:

> Marriage, according to God's design, to which we are *recalled by our Lord Jesus Christ,** is the lifelong union of one man and one woman, to the exclusion of all others on either side.

They set forth the purposes of marriage and the necessity of proper consent. The Commission then recommended the elimination of the Matthean Exception on the grounds of its "doubtfulness . . . the extreme difficulty of determining the innocence of either party to a divorce, and of maintaining the disciplinary safeguards of our existing Canon, and the confusion which these introduce into the Church's law." In the judgment of this Commission "the wise course is to refuse the Church's rites of benediction upon any marriage after divorce, during the lifetime of the other party to the original marriage." The Commission also proposed the canonical recognition of the doctrine of nullity "for causes arising before the marriage" and said that a Decree of Divorce given on such grounds "being in fact, a Decree of Annulment, is no bar to the marriage of either party," but they felt that *"satisfactory evidence** touching the facts in the case, including a copy of the Court's Decree and record, if practicable, with proof that *the defendant was personally served** or appeared in the action," should be required by the Ecclesiastical Authority.[4]

This Report was considered first by the House of Deputies. The elimination of the Matthean Exception was voted upon

---

*Italics mine.
[4] See *Journal of the General Convention* 1916, p. 501 ff. Bps. Cheshire, A. C. A. Hall, F. Burgess, C. P. Anderson, and Mr. F. C. Morehouse signed this Report.

separately from the rest of the Report and the recommendation of the Commission was defeated by a narrow margin. The vote by orders was in the clerical order 40½ in the affirmative; negative 24¾; divided 8; in the lay order—affirmative 29; negative 32¾; divided 6.[5]

The other recommendations of this Report were withdrawn and the Commission continued.

The Commission in 1919 renewed its recommendations to eliminate the Matthean Exception but the House of Deputies again turned it down. The matter apparently was not considered in 1922, except that the canonical prohibition forbidding clergy to solemnize the marriages of divorced persons was extended so as to enjoin members of this Church from entering upon such marriages. This addition obviously was already implicit in our canon law. The Matthean Exception continued to be recognized, for this amendment did not make any changes on that issue.

2. From 1925—1946.

The General Convention of 1925 apparently marked an important turning point in the history of marriage legislation in our Church. Two serious setbacks were suffered by the forces in this General Convention which were working for the principle of indissolubility.

One was the rejection of the Petition of the Sanctity of Marriage Association, which asked the General Convention to adopt a canon on marriage similar to the proposals of the 1916 Commission.[6]

The other was the sidestepping of the Minute or Statement on Marriage and Divorce offered by Bishop Guerry of South Carolina. This Minute read, in part, as follows:

[5] *Id.*, p. 233.
[6] See *Journal of the General Convention* 1925, pp. 217, 225, 259.

We the Bishops of the Church recognize that we have a responsibility to discharge in the matter of upholding the sanctity and the integrity of the marriage relation, and having in view the growing scandal of divorce in our Country, desire to place ourselves on record as favoring a stricter interpretation of the teachings of Holy Scripture touching the indissolubility of the marriage bond than that which underlies the existing Canon.* We wish to affirm that while the law of the State regards marriage as a civil contract, this Church in the office of Holy Matrimony in her Book of Common Prayer holds that it is a lifelong relationship instituted by Almighty God and not to be annulled by cruelty, desertion, marital infidelity or for any cause arising after wedlock.

In common with the teaching of Holy Scripture and of the most enlightened Sociology of the day we declare that the family is the unit of Society and not the individual. In the application of this fundamental principle of our Social Order to domestic conditions it will often happen that the happiness of the individual will have to be sacrificed to the welfare of Society.

We further realize that in order to protect the innocent from the guilty, and the weak from the cruelty and rapacity of the strong, conditions may arise which will make a legal separation . . . both necessary and desirable. . . . The marriage bond is not broken and the door of forgiveness and reconciliation is still open.

Furthermore, we deplore all hasty and ill-advised marriages . . . we call upon all parents, guardians and teachers to instruct those committed to their charge and more particularly the youth of the Church as to the sacramental nature of the marriage relation and also as to what constitutes Christian marriage with its solemn obligations and responsibilities.

This Minute was placed on the calendar and made a Special Order of business for 8 p.m. of the 13th Day. It is said by an

---
*Italics mine.

unofficial source[7] that Bishop Brent had agreed to support Bishop Guerry in this matter, but as the resolution came up for consideration after supper, which was not a very propitious time for so important a question, Bishop Brent, most unfortunately, was not present in the House.

Bishop Page of Michigan offered a substitute resolution for Bishop Guerry's Statement calling for a Joint Commission "to study the whole problem of Divorce, its conditions and causes,[8] and report to the next General Convention." This was unfortunately adopted.[9] It seems to be the general tendency of both Houses of the General Convention to do this, when suddenly confronted with a far-reaching problem even though the principle involved may be clearly stated by the Book of Common Prayer, which is a part of the Constitution of the Church. In this case, the principle of Bishop Guerry's Statement is the same as that of the Marriage Service of the Prayer Book.[10]

Bishop Page was made Chairman of this Commission; also the Bishops of New Jersey and South Carolina were appointed. It is significant to note, because of his views on the subject (see *post* p. 135), that Bishop Scarlett (then the Rev. Dr. Scarlett of Missouri) was appointed to serve from the House of Deputies.[11]

When this Commission made its report in 1928, Bishop Guerry having died in June of that year, the tide had obviously turned and was now running toward the Roman Catholic doctrine of extended nullity and the conception of Eastern Ortho-

---

[7]This information was supplied by the late Rev. Sumner Guerry, the Bishop's son.

[8]Referring to this Resolution Dr. Gwynne asks: "Can any one imagine Ignatius, Bishop of Antioch, or Iranaeus of Lyons, in the second century, or Chrysostom of Constantinople in the fourth, appointing a commission to make a careful research of 'conditions and causes of divorce' in the Roman Empire, in order that, as Bishops in the Church of God, they might know what to do about it?" (*Holy Matrimony and Common-Sense*, p. 50.)

[9]The House of Deputies concurred.

[10]For references on the above, see *Journal of the General Convention* 1925, pp. 92, 93, 117, 121, 122, 312.

[11]*Idem*, p. X.

doxy about the moral and spiritual death of a marriage. This Report said:

> . . . there are those who feel that the Church should be allowed greater freedom of divorce than is allowed at the present time.

The Commission presented a Resolution, which was approved by the General Convention, asking for the continuance of the Commission, using these ominous words: "that it cooperate with other agencies to secure a scientific study of the whole subject of marriage and divorce." (*Journal of the General Convention* 1928, p. 454-5.)

Bishop Davis of Western New York and Dr. F. C. Grant were added to this Commission.

It is important to call attention to the sharp difference in philosophy and approach to this problem between the Commissions of 1916 and 1928. The former emphasized the primary importance of proceeding first of all on the basis of right principles, and then to a consideration of the proper kind of canonical legislation which should be enacted. The latter adopted definitely the humanistic approach. Their idea was to continue with a study of divorced couples—in other words, to consider, in cooperation with secular agencies, hard and unfortunate cases, having uppermost in mind the unhappiness of individuals; and then work out a canon on that basis. It cannot be done. In fact, if the right solution to this problem (and we do not think it is) is to consider primarily the happiness and contentment of the individual partners to a marriage apart from family obligations, then the best thing to do is honestly to adopt the Lutheran and Protestant views and do away entirely with canonical legislation, leaving the matter to the discretion of parish priests. It is an ancient maxim: "hard cases make poor law."

The study and effort of the Commission[12] should have centered on the historic doctrine of the Anglican Communion on marriage for obviously there has existed, especially since 1925, a fundamental conflict of principle between the School of Divorce and the School of Indissolubility.

From 1928 to 1946 a new philosophy dominated the reports of the Commission, which can be best described as an expression of the extreme individualism of Protestantism, and which can be summarized as follows:

(1) Our Lord's teaching on divorce is not legislative, and therefore is not an application of a divine law governing family relationships.

(2) While divorce is a moral calamity, our Lord's words on the subject are to be considered as an ideal or a counsel of perfection.

(3) Those who have failed in marriage should be forgiven, even though this forgiveness overlooks the habitual sin of adultery and seeks to dispense one from the obligation of an indissoluble relationship.

(4) The so-called doctrine of extended nullity is advanced for acceptation by members of the Commission.

(5) Education for marriage is the only real solution for the evil of divorce.

---

[12] Bishop Guerry of South Carolina was a member of this Commission, yet this 1928 Report made no reference to his views, only saying: "On the soul of no man did the subject of divorce lie more heavily than on that of Bishop Guerry. He travelled long distances to attend meetings and our Report owes much to his earnest counsel and help. One of his last acts was to send a check for the work of the Commission."

Dr. Gwynne, however, has recorded Bishop Guerry's views concerning the position of this Commission: "On February 23, 1928, and again on May 30, only ten days before his tragic death on June 9, Bishop Guerry wrote me his unchanged convictions as to our Lord's teaching concerning marriage and, at the same time, his fears that he stood alone in this respect on the Joint Commission." (*Holy Matrimony and Common-Sense*, p. 52.)

Dr. Gwynne also says of the Report of this Commission that the authority of our Lord, the "noblest of all teachers," is "never once directly appealed to." (*Holy Matrimony and Common-Sense*, p. 40. This book provides a good historical sketch of this subject during the period 1808-1928. The author gives a great many details; e.g., the General Conventions of 1808 and 1868.)

(6) The family, even though the fundamental unit of society, should not have priority over the happiness of partners to a marriage.

These constituted in general the type of answers which most of the members of the Joint Commissions on Marriage and Divorce gave to the questions involved in this difficult matter.[13]

1931—The Commission in its 1931 Report said that it is *"easily possible to extend the principle of annulment to cover all sorts of mental and moral deficiencies that existed in people before marriage."** For the increasing evil of divorce, they offered a new Canon (1931), which would have allowed the remarriage[14] of divorced persons at the discretion of an ecclesiastical court, but this particular proposal was rejected by the General Convention.

However, a new and, on the whole, an improved Canon was adopted; its only real weakness being the retention of the Matthean Exception and the provision of Dr. Robbins *et al.* (See *supra*, footnote 14.) The doctrine of nullity, as implied in the Book of Common Prayer in the Marriage Service, was written into the American Canon for the first time, the list of impediments being practically the same as our present Canon, except for impediments 8 and 9,[15] which were added in 1946. (*Journal of the General Convention* 1931, pp. 476, 300.)

1934—The Commission's Report revealed that the same philosophy of divorce prevailed:

> ... the outstanding value of the present Canon lies in its emphasis on education for marriage ... *the only hope of sanctifying marriage is by an educative process** The

---

[13]See *supra*, p. 34.

*Italics mine.

[14]Bp. Matthews, Dr. Stetson and Dr. H. C. Robbins of the Commission dissented from this proposal and substituted the very unfortunate back-door provision for a blessing of such a union afterwards by a priest of our Church. This was made a part of the Canon of 1931.

[15]*Supra*, p. 13.

Western Church has worked under the present restrictive Canon for centuries but nevertheless the divorce rate continues to increase all over the world. . . . (*Journal of the General Convention,* 1934, p. 481.)

In other words, they seem to imply in this statement that the most important thing to consider is the manner in which the divorce rate has increased. The hardness of the hearts of men against the will of God is not stressed. The disobedience of man is certainly not a test as to whether or not a "restrictive canon" expresses the mind of God in Christ.

It is significant to note that Dr. B. S. Easton, because of his conclusions on this issue,[16] had been added to the membership of the Commission.

This General Convention adopted only one canonical change, i.e., a modification of the three-day rule. This required that the intention of the parties to contract a marriage be signified to the minister at least three days before the service; ". . . for weighty cause . . . one of whom is a member of his own congregation" (Canon of 1934), the minister is allowed to dispense with this requirement.

1937—The Commission again seemed to disregard the historic Anglican doctrine of marriage. They granted that the lifelong union of married couples is God's standard and is in accord with the Christian ideal; that divorce is sin caused by hardness of heart; that the Church must maintain Christ's standard of marriage, saying:

> There can be no difference in opinion about this but there is a difference of opinion as to how far punitive methods are effective in the Church. . . . They[17] know that Christ came into the world to forgive sinners; but they nowhere find that He withheld forgiveness alone from

---
[16]*Supra,* p. 37.
[17]I.e., Christians.

those who committed adultery or from the divorced, who were remarried.[18] (*Journal of the General Convention*, 1937, pp. 480, 477.)

The problem, however, is how adulterers can be forgiven without repentance and as long as they continue to live in adultery, forsaking a former spouse.

The Commission proposed an amendment, which renewed their effort of 1931, to grant to our Bishops the authority, at their discretion, to permit the remarriage of divorced persons. Dr. H. C. Robbins dissented from this recommendation: "(1) On Scriptural grounds as tending to weaken the witness of the Church to the Christian ideal of marriage; (2) on constitutional grounds as giving Bishops ecclesiastical power to set aside at their discretion canonical requirements defined by the General Convention."

This proposal of the Commission was overwhelmingly defeated.

To quote again from their Report (Bishop Page speaking):

> There are those who would stiffen the present Canon by omitting the Exception in favor of adultery and never allow remarriage. . . . *The objection to this method is that it has failed.** Only fifty years ago it was practically the attitude of our whole Western civilization. Even where divorce and remarriage were recognized by law they were looked upon with horror. The English Church and some of its Branches[19] have uncompromisingly held this position —the only so-called Catholic Church to do so, yet its leading layman[20] has recently married a twice divorced woman.

---

[18]Sentimentalism concerning this complicated problem of marriage and divorce is actually dangerous to the welfare of society. "The sentimentalist", writes Dean Inge, "is kind only to be cruel, and unwittingly promotes precisely the results he most deprecates." (Quoted in Gwynne's *Holy Matrimony and Common-Sense*, p. 196.)

*Italics mine

[19]All of its Branches except the American Episcopal Church.

[20]It is amazing that King Edward VIII, who abdicated his trust and responsibility as England's reigning sovereign for marriage with a woman already twice divorced, should be considered as the leading layman of the English Church!

... To most Anglicans and Protestants it[21] seems nothing but divorce under another name. ... Another difficulty with annulment is that our studies in education and psychology make it clear that the character attributes which wreck marriage have been formed before marriage; and it will be increasingly difficult to lay down canon laws that will apply to all reasonable grounds for annulment on the basis of 'cause arising before marriage.' (*Journal of the General Convention*, 1937, p. 474-5.)

1940—The Commission offered an amended marriage canon, which omitted the Matthean Exception, but suggested no radical change of principle. In fact, this proposal contained a clear requirement that the impediments listed should be in existence "at the time of the marriage" on the basis of which "the Bishop may declare the marriage ecclesiastically null."

The impediments set forth in this proposed canon were practically the same as in the Canon now in force, except that impediment No. 4, which was a questionable suggestion, was proposed to read: "Mental deficiency . . . sufficient to prevent fulfilment of the marriage vows." In his comment on this Dr. Robbins said: "We have removed 'insanity' because in law it has a very limited meaning. We have inserted No. 4 as covering also those personality deficiencies which make a successful marriage impossible—such as habitual alcoholism, arrested development, mental and emotional, etc."[22]

Also they suggested that the blessing of divorced persons who have been remarried outside of the Church should be retained.

A redraft of this new Canon embodying practically the same features of the Commission's Report was adopted by the House of Bishops but was rejected by the House of Deputies.

1943—The Commission's Report stated that sixty-four Dio-

---
[21]Namely, annulment.
[22]*Journal of the General Convention* 1940, p. 480.

cesan Committees had been appointed to study the question of marriage and divorce and make suggestions. The Report said:

> If a physical defect, which prevents physical consummation of the marriage, makes the marriage voidable, then, from the point of view of the Church, a spiritual defect, which prevents spiritual consummation, should make it voidable. No one questions annulment on the ground of insanity or feeblemindedness, but there are certain abnormalities and defects of character which, while not so discernible before marriage, are nevertheless just as real and insurmountable obstacles to a true marriage as mental incapacity. . . . Canon B proposes to put into the hands of the diocesan bishops the right to decide when this is the case.

After a reference to the impediments, the Report continues:

> We proceed to the general area of such impediments as psychic impotence . . . which were in existence at the time of the contract and could effectively prevent the fulfilment of the marriage vows. . . . We go on to deteriorations or incapacities due to factors which, although latent at the time of the marriage, are brought into actuality by situations inherent in marriage itself.[23]

This majority Report of the Commission was finally presented for enactment in the form of the Phister Amendments[24] which amounted to a simplified expression of the majority's proposal concerning the remarriage of divorced persons. These were defeated in the House of Deputies.

The Proposed Canon, as presented by the Commission (1943),

---

[23] *Journal of the General Convention* 1943, p. 437.

[24] These were proposed by a minority of the Committee on Canons to which Committee the Commission's Report had been referred. The vote by orders was lost by a narrow margin: Clerical—Ayes, 38¾; noes, 31¼; divided 9. Lay—Ayes, 45¼; noes, 24½; divided, 4 (*Id.*, p. 254). In the General Convention a divided vote counts as a negative vote. A vote by orders requires a majority vote in both orders; so the above vote was lost in the clerical order. *Id.*, pp. 252, 254.

incorporated the philosophy of the above statements made by this Commission; e.g.:

> If the Bishop finds that the former contract could not be the spiritual union taught by Christ because of (a) the existence of any of the impediments specified . . . (b) the existence of abnormalities or deficiencies of character sufficient to prevent the fulfilment of the marriage vows, or (c) the existence of an irremediable mental, moral or spiritual deterioration or incapacity, *the causes of which were latent before the previous contract and exposed by the marital relationship** . . . he shall grant the applicant's request.

This proposed Canon was obviously an effort to extend the doctrine of nullity so as to include divorce *a vinculo matrimonii*. (For the record of the above Reports and events see the *Journal of the General Convention*, 1943.)

A Note on impediments: the list of impediments to marriage in the Canons of 1931, 1934, 1937, 1940, 1943 are all the same, except that in the Canon of 1937 Impediment 7 was changed to include also sexual perversion, so that it read: "Impotence or sexual perversion of either party undisclosed to the other." The new Canon of 1946 contains the same list of impediments as did the Canon of 1943 except that Impediment 2 (1943)—"Lack of free or legal consent of either party"—was written into Impediment 9 of 1946; and Impediments 7 and 8 (1943) were united into Impediment 6 of 1946. Impediments 8 and 9 of 1946, which are pregnant with opportunities for the use of the so-called doctrine of extended nullity, were added in that year.

It is important to note that the prohibition ordering a minister not to perform the marriage ceremony for a divorced person used the following words according to the Canon of 1943: "*from whom he or she has been divorced for any cause arising*

---

*Italics mine.

HISTORICAL SKETCH OF MARRIAGE LEGISLATION 129

after marriage."* (Canon 17, Section 2—1943.) In 1949 this prohibition was restored after being omitted in 1946, but the reference to "any cause arising after marriage" was left out.

1946—The Commission's Report[25] said that fifty Diocesan Committees had been formed during the triennium to study the question of Holy Matrimony and that the following tracts had been prepared at the request of the Commission and distributed to these committees: "The N. T. on Marriage" (Divorce and the N. T.) by Dr. B. S. Easton; "Notes on the History of Marriage Legislation" by F. A. Pottle of Yale; "The Mind of Christ on Marriage" by Dr. F. C. Grant; "The Theological Aspect of Christian Marriage" by W. Norman Pittenger, S.T.M.; "Jesus' Teaching on Divorce" by Dr. S. E. Johnson.

The Commission expressed its views in the following manner:

> ... her[26] legislation should aim not only in keeping married people together but ... in case of utter marital failures in helping to build *new and better homes*.* This last entails a canon flexible enough to enable the Church to deal with individual cases of divorce upon their merits. ... Christ's teaching was that *in a God-made marriage a lifelong bond is created*.* ... It is similar to 'the mystical union that is betwixt Christ and his Church'. ... *Christ's teaching is not a law*;* nor is it an ethical precept; it is a statement of fact ... the criterion of a true marriage lies in the parties' consent of heart, mind, and will. If such consent is not given by reason of spiritual, mental, or physical incompetence, or fraud, the indissoluble bond of marriage is not created ... *the words 'free and competent' in the Church's conception must rest upon qualities of the inner man and have a wider meaning than the civil law gives them. With such wider meaning their absence might not be evident until the strains of married life bring them to the surface.* ... *A marriage in which ... there is a hidden*

---
*Italics mine.
[25]*Journal of the General Convention* 1946, p. 442 ff.
[26]I.e., The Church.

or disastrous weakness of character, not evident at the time but manifest later on—a ceremony can not make such a union a true marriage* in the Church's conception.

We note here the tendency to concede the historic principle of indissolubility and then to propose a practice which would in reality repudiate it and actually accept the principle of divorce *a vinculo matrimonii.* Bishop C. J. Davis of Western New York was Chairman of the Commission in 1943 and 1946.

We have already dealt with the events of the General Conventions of 1946 and 1949, and the confusion in the Church which has resulted.[27] Therefore, we are back once more to the present situation in the Church. (It is to be noted that the Canon of 1946 eliminated the Matthean Exception, which was right and proper.)

To summarize the events of 1925—1946: there was an unrelenting effort by one-sided Commissions, being dominated more or less in their thinking by Bishop Page, Bishop Davis, Bishop Scarlett, Dr. Easton and Dr. Grant, to achieve the enactment of a canon which would permit the remarriage of divorced persons for causes arising after the creation of a true and valid bond of marriage. Certainly, it is true to say that these Commissions were not well-balanced or truly representative. The School of Indissolubility had very little participation in their work.

APPENDIX

For references not given above see the Journals of the General Convention: 1901, pp. 75, 132; 1904, pp. 87, 121, 273; 1910, pp. 140, 389; 1913, pp. 93, 244; 1919, pp. 354, 563; 1922, pp. 82, 307, 397; 1931, pp. 125 ff., 350, 486; 1937, p. 473; 1940, pp. 213, 477, 479.

---

*Italics mine.
[27]See *supra*, pp. 15-17.

CHAPTER V

THE NEED FOR A STATEMENT ON THE INDISSOLUBILITY OF MARRIAGE ACCORDING TO THE DOCTRINE AND DISCIPLINE OF THE ANGLICAN COMMUNION

THE NEED FOR A STATEMENT ON THE INDISSOLUBILITY OF MARRIAGE ACCORDING TO THE DOCTRINE AND DISCIPLINE OF THE ANGLICAN COMMUNION

WE have seen that what the School of Divorce in the American Episcopal Church was unable to accomplish by a direct assault on the historic Anglican position on marriage, they have finally achieved by the use of the ambiguous language of Canon 18, Section 2(b),[1] under which divergent interpretations of the Canon have been allowed. The Special Committee of the House of Bishops (1949) distinctly said that an interpretation which granted the right of remarriage to a divorced person for causes arising after a former marriage is perfectly permissible. They have not in principle expressly repudiated the doctrine of indissolubility; in fact, they say that "a God-made marriage," whatever that may be as distinguished from other valid marriages, is indissoluble; yet, in actuality, they have approved divorce *a vinculo matrimonii*. They have condoned what our Lord has condemned by acquiescing in the practice of two irreconcilable principles in connection with this Canon dealing with the remarriage of divorced persons; i.e., the principle of divorce *a vinculo matrimonii* versus the principle of the indissolublity of marriage. The fact that the former is described as extended nullity does not alter the case. Permission for the remarriage of a divorced person for a cause arising before a former marriage, such as insanity, fraud, agreement of concubinage etc., which nullifies the consent necessary to the creation of the marriage bond, is the application of the principle of true nullity (See the Marriage Service in the Prayer Book), and is not at all inconsistent with

---
[1]*Supra*, p. 12.

the principle of the indissolubility of marriage, unless it is abused as it was during the Middle Ages.

The House of Bishops (1949) has also acquiesced in the practice and application of these irreconcilable principles concerning the remarriage of divorced persons by not disapproving of that part of the Report of the Special Committee which recognized the principle of divorce *a vinculo matrimonii*. They had a golden opportunity to eliminate some of the confusion now existing in the Church by approving the dissent from this report which was made by the Bishop of New Jersey on the ground "that only one point of view, that of the Doctrine of Nullity, should be in the Canon."[2]

The divergent interpretations of the Canon since 1946 have taken three forms:

1. The Historic Principle of Indissolubility.

Sixty per cent of our Bishops, it is reported[3] follow this principle and also follow a true principle of nullity. This point of view has been ably set forth in *The Marriage Manual* drawn up under the supervision of the Bishop of Long Island. It declares:

> Consanguinity and duress can plainly mean only such as exist *ab initio* and when, in the same catalog, other conditions are enumerated which, standing alone, might conceivably arise after an attempted marriage, it is impossible to interpret the intention of General Convention, in the absence of express statement, to have been that some of the prescribed conditions are to be pre-existent and some may arise after the attempted marriage.[4]

Again, on p. 48, this Manual, after referring to that part of the ambiguous language of Canon 18, Section 2(b), which refers to marriage as "in intention lifelong," says:

---
[2]*Journal of the General Convention* 1949, p. 440.
[3]*Supra*, p. 20.
[4]P. 26.

And other parts of our formularies, especially the Form for Solemnization of Holy Matrimony in the Book of Common Prayer, clearly teach the doctrine of indissolubility. Moreover, the official teaching of the Church of England on this point is even less open to dispute than the teaching of our American Church. We have expressly declared our intention not to depart from our Mother Church on any essential point of doctrine, discipline, or worship, etc. So the term 'lifelong' must receive, in an official document of our Church, the meaning which puts it in harmony with the doctrine of indissolubility, not the meaning which would put it in hopeless conflict with that doctrine and in contradiction to it.[5]

It may rightly be impossible to interpret this Canon otherwise, but, in fact, that is what is being done.

2. The So-Called Principle of Extended Nullity.

See the statements above in the Reports of the Marriage Commission, and also those made by Bishop Conkling and by Bishop Davis. The danger to the principle of the indissolubility of marriage which exists from the application of extended nullity is revealed by the following remarks, which were made by two of our Bishops in the meeting of the House of Bishops in 1947:

> Bishop Scarlett of Missouri: 'We can't ask this House to accept a new doctrine of marriage—I mean the indissolubility of marriage. *We have no such doctrine in this Church.*'* I object to having the causes before marriage the only causes of annulment. . . . The Canon is a compromise; it allows freedom of a Christian's conscience.
>
> Bishop Hobson of S. Ohio: 'If a man or woman goes to Bishop Gardner, and the cause of divorce was adultery, the Bishop of New Jersey would say that the cause happened after marriage. If he or she came to me, I should say that the defect in character, leading to adultery, existed

---
[5] P. 48-49.
*Italics mine.

before marriage. The rulings would be different.' (Both of these quotations are given as reported by *The Living Church*, November 16, 1947.)

3. The Sufficiency of the Intention to enter into a Christian Marriage.

This interpretation, which was put forth by the Chancellor of the Diocese of Michigan, was published in The Witness, February 13, 1947. The Chancellor said:

> I am of the opinion that the Bishop has the power, after making a finding that a true Christian marriage is intended, to grant permission to remarry, *even though none of the impediments named exist or ever existed.**[6]

It can be rightly said that the Church can tolerate *divergent or varying applications of the same principle* having to do with an essential point of doctrine, discipline and worship, etc., but most surely *the Church can not allow the existence of divergent interpretations of a Canon which involve the recognition of a principle directly contrary to our Book of Common Prayer.* This, in effect, is a repudiation of the teaching of the Prayer Book.

Our problem, therefore, is fundamentally a conflict of irreconciliable principles and is not a mere matter of practice and administration.

What is needed, therefore, is either an authoritative interpretation (higher than on a diocesan level) or clarifying canonical changes. We actually need both.

If we had in the American Episcopal Church a Supreme Ecclesiastical Court with power to interpret the canons of the Church in harmony with the Constitution of the Church (which includes the Prayer Book), and to hear appeals from Provincial

---
*Italics mine.
[6]See Canon 17, Section 2(b).

and Diocesan Courts on matters affecting the entire life of the Church, the problem of the proper interpretation of Canons 17 and 18 could be laid before such a tribunal. Such a Court would have power to declare legislative errors of the General Convention unconstitutional; its interpretations of canonical law would be final and authoritative.

There seems to exist, however, no restraint or check which can be used to control or limit the power of our General Convention. This is a most unfortunate defect in our American Church polity, and out of harmony with the system of checks and balances concerning power, which is normal in the usual forms of democratic and constitutional government. There is no good reason why such a court should not be set up. Also, the veto power, subject to the requirement of a two-thirds majority in both Houses of the General Convention for the passage of a canon over a veto, should be given to our Presiding Bishop.

In 1916 the House of Bishops adopted a Resolution which approved the Report of the Committee on Amendments to the Constitution as the judgment of the House on fundamental principles of constitutional and canonical construction. (The House of Deputies apparently did not act on this.) We know of no later change in this judgment of the House of Bishops. The Report of the Committee said:

> The General Convention differs from Congress and State Legislatures (so far as constitutional limitations are concerned) in that we have no 'Supreme Court' charged with the prerogative of deciding whether a canon is constitutional or unconstitutional. Consequently, the duty of deciding whether a canon (whether proposed or already enacted) is constitutional or not, is a prerogative which devolves upon the General Convention itself, and its decision in such regard is final. . . . It is inconceivable that any session of the General Convention would intentionally pass

a Canon contradicting an express provision of the Constituition. . . .⁷

So the only court of appeal to which we can go is the General Convention itself. It is difficult to see how the same body can exercise both legislative and judicial powers; but, nevertheless, this happens to be the case.

Important as it is to secure clarifying canonical changes in regard to Canons 17 and 18, it is even more important for the General Convention to adopt a statement on the Anglican doctrine of Marriage, so as to clear up the confusion in the Church. The present Commission of the General Convention on Matrimony is the proper authority to propose this. They should follow the example of the Commission of 1916, who thought it best "to agree on certain principles, which should regulate any legislation concerning marriage."⁸ Such a statement could use as a basis for a proper declaration of principles the Marriage Service in the Book of Common Prayer, the statement of the 1916 Commission, the Report of the Archbishops' Commission,⁹ the interpretation by Mr. Justice Vaisey,¹⁰ the declarations of the Lambeth Conferences, leaving out of course the references of Lambeth which approve the Matthean Exception.¹¹

We remember that at the General Convention of 1946 there was confusion and much disagreement on the subject of union with the Presbyterian Church in the U. S A. In order to clear up this confusion, it was proposed by this General Convention that a statement of faith and order in harmony with the Lambeth Quadrilateral be drawn up by the Joint Commission on Approaches to Unity. This declaration, concerning essential principles, was afterwards drawn up by the Commission. It

---
⁷*Journal of the General Convention* 1916, pp. 91, 92.
⁸*Supra*, p. 116.
⁹*Supra*, p. 99.
¹⁰*Supra*, p. 97.
¹¹*Supra*, p. 108.

received the stamp of approval from the Lambeth Conference (1948) and was adopted by the General Convention of 1949 by an overwhelming, if not unanimous, vote. We believe that the same can be accomplished concerning the Anglican doctrine of marriage.

Such a statement, presented in the form of a resolution, should be primarily based on the Marriage Service in the Book of Common Prayer, so that if it is not adopted by the General Convention its action would amount to a repudiation of the Prayer Book's doctrine of marriage.

If it is approved by the General Convention, then the Commission should have ready, for immediate consideration, such canonical changes as would remove the ambiguous language of Canon 18, Section 2 (b). Thus the confusion now existing in the Church would be dispelled.

APPENDICES

A. THE ADMISSION OF DIVORCED PERSONS TO HOLY BAPTISM, CONFIRMATION, AND HOLY COMMUNION

B. THE PASTORAL CARE OF THE BISHOP UNDER CANON 18, SECTION 2(b)

A. THE ADMISSION OF DIVORCED PERSONS TO HOLY BAPTISM, CONFIRMATION AND HOLY COMMUNION

THE problem here is essentially a disciplinary one concerning the status of divorced persons who have remarried outside of the Church, and then request admission to the Sacraments. Under Canon 16, Section 3 (a), ministers of this Church are automatically required to refer such a person to the Bishop for his godly judgment thereupon "before receiving such persons to these ordinances". If this does not mean automatic excommunication for communicants of our Church who have "married otherwise than as the word of God and discipline of this Church" allows, then it is certainly the equivalent, for the minister is required to take positive action.

Thus the Church is confronted with an accomplished fact. The application of the parties for admission to Holy Communion or the other Sacraments poses a difficult problem. They are usually people who live in a society in which divorce *a vinculo matrimonii* is legalized and recognized, so they have no strong remorseful feeling that their relationship is wrong or sinful.

In July 1937 *The Living Church* published my article entitled, "Shall the Church permit Remarriage after Divorce?" Afterwards a clergyman in New England wrote these words to me: "Thanks for your article on Divorce. I agree completely. *But what are we to do with the situation as we find it.?** We all find cases where one or both parties are just cut off from religion and Church altogether by their own mistake, I admit; but something constructive ought to be done for them; some-

---
*Italics mine.

thing that will not do more harm than good. *Write another on what we are to do.**

Canon 16, Section 3(a), continues:

> The Bishop, after due inquiry into the circumstances, and taking into consideration the godly discipline both of justice and mercy, shall give his judgment thereon in writing.

What is "godly discipline both of justice and mercy"? "What are we to do with the situation as we find it?"

Many of our Bishops apparently tend to be very lenient, so much so that a communicant of our Church is often readmitted to Holy Communion only a few months following remarriage after divorce outside of the Church. Such leniency breaks down the standard of the indissolubility of marriage, places the Church in a most inconsistent position, and reduces the Church's discipline to a farce. The admission of the Matthean Exception into our canon in 1868 weakened considerably the principle of indissolubility because it has been used as an opening wedge to provide other grounds for divorce. Adultery is not the only serious sin. Likewise, the readmission to Holy Communion of persons who have remarried after divorce, in a short space of time, has brought many in the Church to the point of saying, "If we are going to do this, we might as well marry them in the Church also!"

It is probably safe to say that most parish priests recommend and that most Bishops grant such applications, unless the applicants have been guilty of serious scandalous conduct. It has happened, from time to time, that such divorced persons have sought through readmission to Holy Communion to regain their moral standing in the eyes of the community. Some priests will not refer an application for a considerable length of time, if the

---
*Italics mine.

person, being a communicant of our Church, knowingly and wilfully remarried after divorce.

There seems to be, however, a general feeling throughout the Church that such persons should be kept under the pastoral care of the Church. The Lambeth Conference (1948) in Resolution 95 (under the heading of the Church's Discipline in Marriage) urged "that provincial and regional churches should consider how best their pastoral responsibility towards those who do not conform to our Lord's standard can be discharged." The Encyclical Letter of the same year said:

> When there has been divorce and remarriage, the Church must keep those concerned within its pastoral care and love, recognizing with sympathy and understanding the suffering and distress which have been inflicted upon many of them and desiring for the sinful penitence.

The Lambeth Committee on Marriage (1948), while recognizing the fact of automatic excommunication following remarriage after divorce, said:

> But we also recognize that, when such a marriage has been contracted and the parties to it desire and intend to establish a Christian home, the bishop . . . may authorize their admission to Holy Communion. The bishop's decision must inevitably depend partly on the evidence whether any grave scandal arising out of the divorce or the subsequent remarriage exists.[1]

Of course, everyone would agree that all sinners should be kept under the pastoral care of the Church. But is it right to assume, as so many of us have, and as is implied by the above statement, that such applications, as a general rule, should be granted unless there is "grave scandal" involved in the case?

---
[1] P. 101.

Have we a right to assume that the usual remarriage after divorce in the eyes of God is not "a grave scandal"?

The underlying principle of our Lord's words is the indissolubility of marriage. Hence remarriage after divorce *a vinculo matrimonii* involves continuous adultery. It is a matter of public knowledge and record, and, in applying for Holy Communion, the parties usually have no idea of a repentance which would include giving up their marriage. Therefore, it would seem that if the Church is to be *absolutely* consistent and the Bishop's judgment is to be strictly right and godly, the application should be refused, unless they give up their unlawful marriage or can bring the former marriage under the doctrine of true nullity by proof that one of the impediments in Canon 17 existed at the time of such previous marriage.

Dr. Cirlot is in accord with such a strict application of the Canon:

> The Church would be illogical and inconsistent if she taught that remarriage after divorce is adultery (as loyalty to Christ absolutely requires her to do) and at the same time allowed persons persisting in such remarriage to be communicants in good standing. For by so doing she would clearly imply one of these things: (1) that remarriage after divorce is not adultery; or (2) that adultery is not a grave sin; or (3) that it is possible to make a worthy (and hence profitable) Communion without repenting of grave sin and sincerely purposing to desist from that sin in the future.[2]

There are many, however, who would hold that "godly discipline" means that justice and logic must be tempered with mercy in the application of discipline. *The Southern Churchman*[3] published my article on "Marriage and Divorce" in which

---
[2] *Op. cit.*, p. 178.
[3] May 8, 1937.

I quoted the opinions of several Bishops on this problem. One distinguished Bishop said:

> It does seem to me important that the Church should under present conditions take a firm stand in trying to uphold Christian ideals of marriage, although I think that in the matter of discipline we must take into consideration, as the canon says, both justice and mercy, and that a law which would say that discipline must be lifelong or that parties married contrary to Church law must dissolve their marriage before discipline can be relaxed, while it would be easy, would not be the proper way to deal with the situation. Of course, the danger is that where there is a provision for discretion in discipline that all discipline will go by the board. I am opposed to this.

Also the 1916 Commission said:

> The refusal of the Church to bless and solemnize a marriage need not be followed by a permanent exclusion from the Sacraments.
>
> Consideration must be had of the good faith in which a marriage may have been entered on, in ignorance of the Church's law, and while not subject to the Church's discipline; and of the practical impossibility in many cases, without greater wrong, of the breaking up of a family. In some such cases there must be a power of discretion, *very carefully exercised*,* to admit or readmit persons to the Sacraments. This power must rest with the Minister of the Congregation and the Bishop of the Diocese, as the chief minister of discipline.⁴

It is suggested that the present Commission on Marriage should re-study this problem and recommend canonical changes which would harmonize, in a better way than heretofore has been done, the administration of Canon 16, Section 3(a), with

---
*Italics mine.
⁴*Journal of the General Convention* 1916, p. 503.

the principle of the indissolubility of marriage. Such changes might include:

1. A provision that communicants of this Church who have unlawfully remarried after divorce outside of the Church will not be readmitted to Holy Communion until (1) a period of three to five years shall have elapsed (that is, their application will not be considered until some such period of discipline shall have expired); (2) or unless they can base such an application on the principle of nullity and prove the existence of one of the impediments in existence at the time of a former marriage.

2. Another provision should be included concerning those who have remarried after divorce outside the Church, in ignorance of the Church's law, yet who afterwards seek admission to the rites of Christian initiation. Such a provision should suggest that the Bishop should take this sort of a situation under consideration in giving his godly judgment.

In other words, a distinction should be made between members of the Church who remarry in defiance of Church law and those who do so because of ignorance or when they were not subject to the Church's discipline. Certainly, discipline concerning the former class should be tightened up or "all discipline will go by the board."

B. THE PASTORAL CARE OF THE BISHOP UNDER CANON 18, SECTION 2(B)

Many have expressed the view that the great value of this Canon is that it is not legalistic but pastoral. Nevertheless, this Canon calls for the exercise of a judicial function on the part of the Chief Pastor of a Diocese. He is called upon to judge whether or not, in a certain case, the facts as alleged by the petitioner in his application under Canons 18, Section 2(b), and 17, Section 2(b), are shown to exist or to have existed *ab initio*. In other words, one of the impediments listed must be so clearly proved to have existed at the time of the former marriage as to establish manifestly "that no marriage bond as the same is recognized by this Church exists."

After all, a judicial function includes pastoral oversight. It may be a surprise to some to know that our State and Federal judges exercise, along with their judicial powers, a very decided pastoral care. For example, if a defendant in a trial for murder has no one to defend him, the judge will appoint and even require a member of the bar, as an officer of the Court, to perform this function. If the circumstances are such that the defendant is penniless, he will have to do it without a fee. The pastoral care of the judge covers the interests of all of the parties in a civil or criminal proceeding, including those of society at large.

Because of the importance of a judgment which affects the interests of more than one person, courts hold that *ex parte* evidence is not reliable unless it is corroborated or subjected to the test of cross-examination and rebuttal testimony or unless the defendant fails to appear at the trial after being personally served.

Surely, no less a standard can be expected of a Bishop who is asked to declare solemnly that a former marriage is null and void, and has never existed. *Ex parte* evidence furnished by the applicant is insufficient and unreliable unless tested or unless the other spouse to the former marriage is personally served with a notice of the petition and fails to appear.

Every effort, however, should be made by the Bishop to include in his judicial and pastoral duty, as Chief Pastor, the interests of all of the parties of the former marriage; i.e., both the husband and the wife, and the children.

The survey, as reported in The Saturday Evening Post by Wittels (*supra*, p. 78 ff.), revealed the fact "that most of those shattered marriages and broken homes were needless tragedies. There were no unsolvable basic difficulties in most of the cases."

The indication is, as applied on a national scale, that at least fifty percent of broken marriages could have been prevented "if somebody had stepped in at the right moment and talked sense to them." (*Idem.*)

Because of this factor and because of the assembly line and narrow legalistic procedures of divorce courts,[5] which are based on the idea that the defendant is guilty of cruelty, infidelity, etc., and must be punished by a decree of absolute divorce, leading lawyers and judges want to require that, in all cases in which children are involved, both husband and wife, if possible, must be brought into court and that the State should contest the case or appear on behalf of the Children. "The approach of the Court would be: 'Never mind who did what to whom, can it be straightened out? What is best for him, the children and everybody else?'." Judge Alexander, Chairman of the American Bar Association's Committee on Divorce and Marriage Laws and Family Courts, has said:

> But under our divorce laws we allow the people suffering from sick marriages to prescribe for themselves. We, the judges—transcribe that as 'doctors'—must sit there and be guided by their own biased diagnosis. How silly! We let the patient tell us that the terrible surgery of divorce is the only cure. In many of the thousands of divorce cases in which I theoretically sat as a judge I wasn't able to be a judge at all. I was more of a mortician. To scramble the metaphor further, it was as if all a doctor was allowed to do was to issue death certificates. *In my heart I know I've been forced to bury many live marriages.** (Wittels' fifth article, "Perjury Unlimited," February 18, 1950.)

Our reference to this series of articles by no means indicates

---

[5] It is reported by Wittels that eighty-five or ninety per cent of all divorce cases are not contested and that in Detroit the average time for the trial of such a divorce case is six minutes.

*Italics mine.

that we think that a Bishop is permitted to proceed under Canon 18, Section 2(b), according to the principle of divorce *a vinculo matrimonii*. It does, however, show that when he proceeds according to the principle of true nullity, he should consider the interests of all of the parties to the former marriage; a need which is indicated most forcibly by Wittels' statements.

Since under Canon 18 the marriages of applicants have already been annulled or dissolved by a civil court, it would probably be too late in most cases for the Bishop to effect a reconciliation. Surely, however, he ought to try to do so. He should attempt to contact all of the parties involved before pronouncing judgment.

Mr. Clifford P. Morehouse introduced an amended Canon 18, Section 2(b), in the General Convention of 1949 which provided that the other party to a former marriage must be notified by the Bishop of the application of a petitioner for remarriage so that *ex parte* evidence could be tested, but the House of Deputies turned it down on the recommendation of the Committee on Canons, who said that this amendment was "impractical and cumbersome."[6]

May be it is, but we see no other reliable manner in which a judgment of nullity can be safely given, unless the Bishop requires a copy of the record of the civil court, and in it there is satisfying evidence as to the existence of the impediment. Such evidence is an indispensable foundation upon which to predicate a sound and godly judgment.

This is a very important matter and should be thoroughly considered by the present Commission on Matrimony so that the proper canonical changes can be effected.

---
[6] *Journal of the General Convention* 1949, p. 170.

BIBLIOGRAPHY

Cirlot,* Felix L.: *Christ and Divorce*, Lexington, Ky., Trafton Publishing Co., 1945.
DeWolfe, James P.: *A Marriage Manual*, New York, Morehouse-Gorham Co.,* 1947.
DuBose, William Porcher: *The Reason of Life*, New York, Longmans, Green, and Co.,* 1911.
Dummelow, J. R.: *The One Volume Bible Commentary*, New York, The MacMillan Co.,* 1913.
Encyclopaedia Britannica,* 1951.
Gwynne, Walker: *Divorce in America under State and Church*, New York, The MacMillan Co.,* 1925; *Holy Matrimony and Common-Sense*, New York, Longmans, Green, and Co.,* 1930.
Gore, Charles:
    (1) *The Creed of a Christian*, London, Wells, Gardner Darton & Co.,* 1895.
    (2) *The New Commentary on Holy Scripture*, New York, The MacMillan Co.,* 1928.
    (3) *The Sermon on the Mount*, London, John Murray,* 1905.
    (4) *The Question of Divorce*, New York, C. Scribner's Sons, 1911.
Joyce, George H., S. J.: *Christian Marriage*, New York, Sheed and Ward, Inc.,* 1933.
Lacey, T. A.: *Marriage in Church and State*, London, Robert Scott, 1912; Revised Edition by R. C. Mortimer; London, S. P. C. K.,* 1947.
Kirk,* Kenneth E.: *Marriage and Divorce*, London, Hodder and Stoughton, 1948.
Marshall,* John S.: *Hooker's Polity in Modern English*, Sewanee, Tenn., The University Press, 1948.
MacMillan, A. T.: *What is Christian Marriage?*, London, The MacMillan Co.,* 1944.
Watkins, O. D.: *Holy Matrimony*, London, Rivington, Percival and Co.,* 1895.
Westermarck, Edward: *History of Human Marriage*, The MacMillan Co.,* 1921.
Tyson, Stuart L.: *The Teaching of our Lord as to the Indissolubility of Marriage*, Sewanee, Tenn., The University Press, 1909.
Wilson, Frank E.: *The Divine Commission*, New York, Morehouse-Gorham Co.,* This is copyright 1940 by the National Council Protestant Episcopal Church.
The Five Lambeth Conferences 1867-1908, London, S. P. C. K.. The MacMillan Co., 1920.
The Conference of Bishops of the Anglican Communion 1920.
Lambeth Conference 1930.
The Lambeth Conference 1948, London, S. P. C. K.
Journals of the General Convention.
Bulletins of the Sanctity of Marriage Association.
Pamphlets printed for the Joint Commission of the General Convention on Marriage and Divorce and written by Dr. B. S. Easton, Dr. F. A. Pottle of Yale, Dr. B. H. Jones, Dr. F. C. Grant; also "An Introduction to the Study of Canon 41" by Frank Gavin, John M. Glenn, Charles C. Marshall, and Howard C. Robbins.
Magazines:
    The Living Church.*
    The Southern Churchman.
    The Witness.*
    The Anglican Theological Review.*
    The Saturday Evening Post;* January and February 1950: "The Post Reports on Divorce" by David G. Wittels.
The San Francisco Chronicle.*
A pamphlet 1949: "A Critique of the Proposals on Marriage and Divorce" by Ralph E. Coonrad* et al.

---

*Authors and publishers whose names are marked with an asterisk have expressly granted permission for the use of the quotations in this book.